Praise for *A Light in the Dark*

"These three authors have thoughtfully built upon the body of knowledge of developmental trauma and adult children of alcoholics to offer the ACSA an in-depth understanding of the unique experiences of growing up in a family impacted by sex addiction. *A Light in the Dark* offers adult children not only a framework and language to understand their experiences but, equally important, a voice and path to their recovery. By recognizing and addressing the consequences of sexual shame, they will forge a new path free of their families' fear, pain, and shame. This book shines light on the dark while providing light for the future. This is an exciting contribution to the recovery field that is much needed and long overdue."

—**Claudia Black, PhD,** author of *It Will Never Happen to Me*, pioneer, adult children of alcoholics movement

"*A Light in the Dark* is a book whose time has come—a beautiful testimonial and guidebook for adult children of sex addicts (ACSAs) raised in the accompanying deceit and chaos of addiction. The authors' unvarnished, firsthand accounts delineate the characteristics common to ACSAs, then deliver the reader to the necessary steps for healing and recovery. This book is, indeed, 'a light in the dark,' illuminating the way for those who've suffered the childhood pains of growing up in a sexually addicted system. A must read for ACSAs and anyone who works in the field of addiction!"

—**Alexandra Katehakis, PhD,** author of *Sex Addiction as Affect Dysregulation: A Neurobio⁻ ⁻⁻ Informed Holistic Treatment*

"Finally, a distinct, expertly informed guide to understanding the impact sexual addiction has on adult children. For too long, adults who grew up in homes with a parent who was sexually addicted have lived without clear language, concepts, and tools to help them understand their experience, reduce their shame, and change their relational patterns. *A Light in the Dark* provides a helpful guide out of the fog of this previously neglected phenomenon into clarity and healing."

—**Michelle Mays, LPC, CSAT-S**, author of *The Aftermath of Betrayal* and *When It All Breaks Bad: Ten Things to Do (and Not to Do) After Betrayal*

"*A Light in the Dark: The Hidden Legacy of Adult Children of Sex Addicts* shines a bright path to hope and freedom from the shame caused by a parent's sex addiction. Written specifically for, and exclusively through, the eyes of adult children of sex addicts, this book is unique in its approach and offers readers a chance to unburden a shameful legacy. Authors Adams, Meyer, and Vande Garde outline the characteristics, roles, and recovery that guide the adult child of a sex addict into a personalized path of healing. This book is certain to become a welcomed resource for both adult children of sex addicts and the clinicians who treat them."

—**John C. Friel and Linda Diane Olund Friel,** licensed psychologists and *New York Times* bestselling authors of *Adult Children: The Secrets of Dysfunctional Families* and *The 7 (Best) Things Happy Couples Do*

"In *A Light in the Dark,* three authors courageously write their own stories of being a child of a sex addict. Excellently written, this book is a first in the field of sex addiction and trauma. The effects of intergenerational trauma, which include but are not limited to sexual shame, are explained in a direct yet compassionate way. Especially important, this book clearly states goals for recovery from being in a sex-addicted afflicted family and how to accomplish healing."

—**Wendy Conquest, MA, LPC, CSAT-S,** author of *Letters to a Sex Addict,* co-author of *Letters from a Sex Addict,* and co-host of the podcast *Conversations on Sex, Addiction and Relationships*

"This book is a game changer for therapists treating addicts as well as recovering adult children of sex addicts. The groundbreaking writing fills a much-needed gap in the literature about sex addiction. As a clinical psychologist, I will be recommending *A Light in the Dark* to both my addicted patients who are parents as well as their children who are hurting."

—**Alyson Nerenberg, PsyD, CSAT-S,** psychologist and author of *No Perfect Love: Shattering the Illusion of Flawless Relationships*

"*A Light in the Dark* is a gift to adult children of sex addicts as well as to the entire treatment community. Sex addiction silently affects the whole family, but often the children within the family are not offered the space or attention to identify the impacts on them. The shared personal stories and clear approaches for healing in this book offer adult children who have been impacted by sex addiction a resource that is validating and supportive, along with offering the much-needed space for them to focus on their pain and find healing."

—**Dr. Piper S. Grant, PsyD, MPH, CSAT,** clinical psychologist and sex therapist

"*A Light in the Dark* may be one of the most important reads for anyone who grew up in a home where infidelity and sexual secrets were common. This book gives a voice to all children who have witnessed sexual betrayal by one or both of their primary caregivers."

—**Dr. Kevin Skinner, LMFT-S, CSAT-S**

"Finally, the book so many parents in recovery have been waiting for—information about the impact of sex addiction on the next generation. With this work, their voices can be heard, and Adams, Meyer, and Vande Garde offer a much-needed resource for spearheading the new era in the recovery field."

—**Janice Caudill, PhD,** author of *Full Disclosure: How to Share the Truth After Sexual Betrayal*

A Light

IN THE DARK

A *Light* IN THE DARK

THE HIDDEN LEGACY OF ADULT CHILDREN OF SEX ADDICTS

Kenneth M. Adams, PhD, Mary E. Meyer, PhD, LMFT, and Culle L. Vande Garde, LCSW

Health Communications, Inc.
Boca Raton, Florida

www.hcibooks.com

Library of Congress Cataloging-in-Publication Data
is available through the Library of Congress

© 2023 Kenneth M. Adams, PhD, Mary E. Meyer, PhD, LMFT, and Culle L. Vande
Garde, LCSW

ISBN-13: 978-07573-2464-2 (Paperback)
ISBN-10: 07573-2464-9 (Paperback)
ISBN-13: 978-07573-2465-9 (ePub)
ISBN-10: 07573-24657-9 (ePub)

Publisher: Health Communications, Inc.
          301 Crawford Boulevard
          Boca Raton, FL 33432-1653

Cover and Interior design by Larissa Hise Henoch

To all the children and adult children
who still carry the burden of sexual shame,
may you become your own
light in the dark.

"Family dysfunction rolls down from generation to generation like a fire in the woods, taking down everything in its path until one person in one generation has the courage to turn and face the flames. That person brings peace to their ancestors and spares the children that follow."

—Terry Real

Contents

Foreword

For those of us with the legacy of sex addiction in the families in which we grew up, we know all too well the devastation, destruction, and heartache this addiction can create for the family. As a child of a parent with sex addiction, I too saw the destruction and wrestled with the trauma and chaos it brought to me and those I love. As a clinician, many years later, I have seen these patterns of trauma and devastation in the many families I have treated. And unfortunately, when sex addiction is discovered, the children are greatly impacted yet rarely receive support or trauma therapy. Many of those children grow up to be adults who still carry unresolved wounding and pain. ACSAs (Adult Children of Sex Addicts) are often left feeling they are carrying their parents' secrets and shame and feel that they cannot tell anyone about the hidden legacy of sex addiction in their family. It is time to end the silence about the pain that we, as ACSAs experience, and to recognize that we too have been impacted and need treatment and support.

The personal stories (provided by the authors, Ken, Mary, and Culle) that open this book are rife with shame—shame that is all too common in the lives of ACSAs. Unfortunately, the shame that we ACSAs feel has kept us quiet for far too long. Unlike adult children of alcoholics, drug addicts, and the mentally ill—issues where social shaming has decreased drastically over the past half century—ACSAs have chosen to suffer in silence, mostly because sexual issues are still taboo and sex addiction is still so misunderstood. So, rather than seeking relief by talking about our feelings, thoughts, and behaviors, our shame has kept us in the closet, so to speak. Our reasoning seems to be: *If you knew about my "sex addiction lineage," you would think about me differently. You would view me as damaged, unworthy, and unlovable.*

Sex and porn addiction is so thoroughly stigmatized that it still flies under the radar, much as we saw with alcoholism and drug addiction one hundred years ago. In other words, sex addiction is viewed as a moral failing, a weakness, and something to be ashamed of rather than a maladaptive coping mechanism (which, ultimately, is what all addictions are). Because of this, sex addicts themselves, with very few exceptions, keep their problem under wraps even while they are in recovery, and their families often keep things even more under wraps.

Sadly, this leaves ACSAs with very few resources and very little support. Nearly always, we walk through life ruled by our shame and negative core beliefs, many (maybe most) of which have *absolutely nothing to do with us*. They are, as Ken, Mary, and Culle note in their introduction and elsewhere in this book, what psychologists refer to as *carried shame*. In other words, the burden of shame that ACSAs carry and that drives so much of our thinking and behavior, even as adults, is not entirely ours. But still, we carry it, and it can impact every aspect of our lives.

The good news is that we needn't do this. Like adult children of alcoholics and drug addicts, we can talk about our situation with others, in particular with other ACSAs, learning from them while also helping them. In time, and together, we can overcome the shame and negative thinking wrought by the knowledge of and the emotional impact of our parents' sexual addiction. We can learn that we no longer need to hide our parents' secrets and carry shame that does not belong to us.

It is important to note here that ACSAs are not the same as adult children of alcoholics. Though similar in many ways, the shame we carry and the negative core beliefs we develop are different. Thus, our problematic adult-life behaviors are also different. Because our parents carried sexual secrets, we often do the same. Because our parents struggled with their relationships, we often feel caught in the middle with divided loyalties. Because we were raised in a sexualized household, we may have received either overly permissive or overly shameful messages about sex and relationships—messages that continue to color our thinking even as adults. Worst of all, we may inadvertently convey these harmful behaviors and messages to our own children—even if we are not ourselves addicted. That is why this book is so important. After decades of trying to get whatever I could from the teachings of

ACOA (Adult Children of Alcoholics) and similar "adult children" programs and books, there is finally a book that speaks to ACSAs directly.

I am very proud of Ken, Mary, and Culle. As someone who has shared my own personal story in many venues, I know that it takes incredible courage. But the validation that ACSAs will experience when reading stories like their own will be invaluable. I'm very grateful to Ken, Mary, and Culle for putting themselves out there and ending the silence so others can also start their healing journey. Their bravery will impact readers on a very deep level. That alone is enough to make this book a must read!

I also can't thank them enough for their extensive and accurate presentation of what it's like to be an ACSA and the work we need to do to heal. First and foremost, of course, they have validated the trauma experienced by children of sex addicts—the conflict of the parents, the role(s) that we get forced into, the split allegiance we feel, not to mention the confusion and fear we experience.

The identification of the characteristics of ACSAs is on point. For those of us who've searched for help previously via Adult Children of Alcoholics and elsewhere, we know that, although we are similar in many ways to ACOAs, we are not the same. We do not share all the same characteristics, and our journey toward overcoming our underlying trauma and harmful adult-life behaviors does not entirely mirror the journey of ACOAs.

This book also recognizes our rights and responsibilities: First and foremost the fact that we must pursue the very specific help we need as ACSAs, not only to heal ourselves, but to prevent ourselves from passing the shame of sexual addiction on to the next generation. We need therapeutic support and peer-focused support that fully understands and focuses on the impact of sexual addiction, knowing that impact is just not the same as with other addictions. Without this assistance, we will continue to suffer, and our children may also suffer.

My father titled his first book *Out of the Shadows*, and this book could easily share that title. Only this time, it is the children of sex addicts rather than the actual addicts who are exiting the dark recesses of shame and entering the healing light of recovery. It's about time too! In fact, we ACSAs are past due for ending the silence and speaking openly about our lives and experiences.

For me, it is an unbelievable honor to write the foreword for this much-needed book. For one thing, Ken, Mary, and Culle are valued and highly respected colleagues and clinicians. They are also, like my father when he wrote *Out of the Shadows*, incredibly brave in pushing themselves and their stories to the forefront. Best of all, they've not done this for glory or to further their already stellar reputations; they've done it to help others with similar backgrounds, thinking, and issues. I have no doubt that through this book and the work to come, they will achieve exactly that.

—**Dr. Stefanie Carnes**

Introduction

Adult children who grew up with a parent who had a sexual addiction are left confused, ashamed, and mistrustful regarding the feelings and boundaries surrounding sex, love, and intimacy. Because of the inappropriate sexual behavior by a parent, and the subsequent impact of betrayal of the other parent, these adults carry sexual secrets, have divided loyalties, and are often caught in the middle of their parents' struggles. Having witnessed (or known of) affairs, walked in on a parent masturbating or viewing pornography, received extreme or shameful messages regarding sexuality or gender, experienced sexualized remarks about their bodies, been neglected as a result of the addiction, or been exposed to extreme moral values (either too permissive or shaming), these Adult Children of Sex Addicts (ACSAs) struggle with their sexuality and longings for love. The burden of shame that they carry is not theirs. This book is written for ACSAs who long to unburden themselves of this shameful legacy and embrace sexuality and intimacy without the intrusion or constraints from the past.

ACSAs have not had their stories told in any significant way in the recovery literature. Their shame and struggle has often been wedged under various umbrellas of identification: adult children of alcoholics, love avoidant, codependent, sex addict, love addict, and others. In order to give ACSAs their own working narrative and to validate their experience, we have stayed away from referencing other models or authors of related topics. We provide references in the bibliography section of the book for those readers who wish to pursue further exploration.

We do borrow the self-help formatting made popular from the Adult Children of Alcoholics (ACOA) literature: characteristics, role identification, and recovery. However, we see the characteristics and roles of ACSAs as significantly different from the ACOA literature. For example, the hero or responsible child identified in the ACOA family is more specifically the Moral Hero and Champion in the ACSA family system. Our observations come from the hundreds of ACSAs that we have seen and treated in our practices over many decades. In addition, we were guided by a previous list of Adult Children of Sex Addicts' characteristics identified by Hunter (1997).

Also, we do not enter the debate as to whether sex can become addictive or not. We align with the growing recognition and evidence that there are individuals who cannot control or stop their compulsive sexual behavior despite the negative consequences that follow. One of the most significant consequences is the shameful legacy left for the children parented by these addicts. The stories and experiences of the ACSAs attest to the reality that sex addiction is real. No individual story we tell in the book is any one client's experience. The stories we present are all composites of the many stories we have heard from the ACSAs we have worked with. Any resemblance to someone's actual family story is merely coincidental and a reflection of the common themes in ACSAs' stories.

Our family examples are heterosexual with the sex addict being male. This has been our primary clinical experience, and we wanted to stay true to what we have observed over our careers. However, it is important to note that women can also be the sexually addicted parent with similar impacts on the children described in our book. Also, same gender couples with families, where one parent is a sex addict, may produce the type of ACSA characteristics and roles we detail. As same-gender couples increasingly emerge as parents, ACSA voices from these families will need to be heard. In addition, the cultural shaming same-gender parents experience may also play a role in inherited shame passed onto the children.

ACSAs who are LGBTQ+ or identify as nonbinary people will need to sort for themselves the characteristics and roles we describe as they relate to their specific circumstances. This way, they can more specifically determine the ways in which their parent's sex addiction have impacted their own unique situations. In time, the voices of LGBTQ+ and nonbinary people who are ACSAs will add to and enrich our understanding of the impact of a parent's sex addiction.

Critical to our book is the concept of intergenerational trauma, whereby one does not need to be directly exposed to trauma to have its impact passed on from a previous generation that was directly affected. Children of Holocaust survivors have been extensively studied and show evidence of the trauma resulting from their parents' horror, even though they were not directly exposed to the Holocaust themselves. Hypervigilance, mistrust, numbing, depersonalization, aloofness, anxiety, and depression are some of the symptoms noted in second-generation trauma survivors. And, there is some suggestion that the third generation may also be impacted.

In the case of the sexually addicted family, intergenerational trauma is transmitted through the legacy of carried sexual shame. ACSAs, being the direct trauma victims of the inappropriate sexual behavior and betrayals, pass on to their offspring the sexual shame they themselves inherited. For example, an ACSA, who has witnessed a parent's affair or lived with constant fighting between the parents over the addict's compulsive pornography use, may become controlling and vigilant regarding sexual matters and messages toward their own children. This next generation, not having been directly exposed to the sex addict's inappropriateness, feels a confusing and unwelcomed shamefulness regarding their own natural sexual curiosity. This second generation, in turn, may become avoidant or permissive sexually as a result of the trauma of intergenerational sexual shame. Our hope is that not only will this book unburden the ACSA but protect a next generation from the impact of sexual shame.

We feel the best way to invite ACSAs to unburden their legacy of sexual shame is by helping them identify and clarify their own stories. We start with sharing ours. The first three chapters tell each of our stories of growing up in sexually addicted families and the journeys we took to find our way. The subsequent chapters identify the ACSAs' characteristics, roles, and recovery that point toward the freedom and joy they rightfully deserve.

—Ken, Mary, and Culle

Chapter One

A Shameful Legacy
I Did Not Ask For—
Ken's Story

The unexpected mail from my uncle contained an accompanying note inside, "Kenny, I thought you should have this letter that came to me. It is about your father. We always knew he was troubled, so I am not surprised by the contents. I hope it is not too disturbing." The letter was from a woman who claimed to be my father's daughter. She stated that, in searching for her biological father, she came upon my uncle. My father had been deceased for twenty years, so his brother was the closest person she could find, given that this daughter was a secret—the result of one of my father's many extramarital affairs.

Shocked but not particularly surprised, due to the rumors over the years of him fathering another child early in our family life, I sat down to take it all in. At first, wanting no part of the painful memories of my father's betrayals, I felt angry with my uncle for sending it. I quickly realized it was not my uncle with whom I was angry but my father.

According to the dates in her letter, I would have been about ten when she was born. I thought back to that time in our family life, and it hit me hard. It was a time when my father was particularly rejecting and dismissive. He wouldn't come home many nights, he would walk out in the middle of holiday dinners, saying he had to go someplace, and he would excessively berate my mother, my brothers, and me. Like the click of a combination lock, the pieces came together, and I began to cry. I felt like that rejected ten-year-old boy all over again. I had no doubt: in rejecting us, he had left the house to be with his affair partner during the pregnancy and the subsequent birth of this daughter.

My name is Ken. I am an adult child of a sexually addicted parent, my father. Having now said that, I feel the immediate shame I have carried most of my life for the legacy of my father's sexual secrets and addictive behaviors. The shame buried itself in me, became my own. I have spent the better part of my life reacting to and defending against that shame. Even now, I am reluctant to share my family's story in any revealing detail because of the shamefulness I feel. Yet I have learned, during my own healing journey, that through sharing I am freed from the burden of shamefulness that is not mine and the legacy I did not ask for.

Long before I read the letter from my father's illegitimate daughter, I had been impacted by his sexual behavior many times. At the age of six, I witnessed my father with another woman during a time my mother was hospitalized for depression, which I now know was caused by her trauma as a result of my father's infidelities and alcoholism. Overwhelmed and confused, I took on a lasting and shameful imprint, knowing he was betraying my mother.

I remember feeling sick in my stomach and protective of my mother. While not understanding fully what being "loyal" meant, I knew what he was doing was wrong and hurtful. He demanded that I keep his secret. I was angry with him and frightened. What I did not know then, but understand more clearly now, was that I too felt I had betrayed my mother by not telling her.

When I was nine, a similar incident of witnessing my father's sex addiction occurred after going to work with him one Saturday. What started out as a proud moment working with my dad turned into yet another shameful and confusing time. He took me to a Chinese restaurant for a meal, and we sat down at a table with the waitress, when he began being amorous with her in front of me. The only reason he stopped was because the waitress stopped him after she saw the apparent shock on my face. Again, he demanded I keep quiet, and again I felt I was keeping secrets from my mother and was complicit in his affairs. For years, Chinese food made me ill, and I could not eat at a Chinese restaurant until later in my adulthood and after years of therapy.

Throughout my entire childhood and youth, my home was a constant source of conflict due to my father's suspected and known infidelities. At night I would hear my parents fighting about his inappropriate sexual behavior. They would also fight when he would not come home at night, my mother no doubt keenly and painfully aware of his whereabouts. He would deny, blame, yell, and create such a conflict that my mother would give up the attempt to confront him, and we would move into a code of silence and "normalization" regarding his behavior. By the time I was nine, I did not believe that kindness, love, or joy were possible. These were all casualties of my father's sex addiction.

All these incidents made it difficult to want to approach girls for a date in high school, as I always felt it was "bad" to be interested. My attraction seemed shameful for some reason; unknowingly, the shame I was feeling then was linked to my father. I spent years being confused by my sexual interest, which left me feeling drawn but hesitant. I had not yet realized that my feelings were occurring in the shadow of my father's addicted and twisted behavior. Fortunately, the shame didn't keep me from having a loving experience with my girlfriend in my last year of high school, which felt innocent and sweet rather than shameful and confusing. While this high school romance did not survive the emerging carried dysfunction and shame of my family, it was nonetheless an oasis in the desert of lost love for me, leaving me always grateful.

Also gaining traction throughout the years was the pity and sorrow I felt for my mother from watching her pain and depression. She would stare out the kitchen window, which allowed her a view of the main road to our house, waiting for my father's car to pull up in the driveway. I would plead with her to make dinner or take care of my brothers and me, but she often seemed frozen in her worry and preoccupation. I would try to make her happy, a role that shouldn't have been mine, but I felt compelled to fill it. I got good grades, would bring her flowers, and one time, I even brought a puppy home for her that I'd found abandoned on the side of the road. On the surface, these all were sweet gestures, but they hid the terrible guilty bind of having to be responsible for my mother. She made no effort to inform me that it was not my job to make her happy.

What made matters worse is that my mother would take advantage of my sorrow for her. I declared loyalty and love to her that was not mine to declare or make up for. I felt guilt when I wasn't tending to her. She would turn to me to complain of her loneliness and to rage about my father and what a bad man he was. She would have me call his workplace and bars to check up on him, not giving any apparent thought to the impact on me. When I was a teen and wanted to be with friends and get out of the house, she would call and check on me; I felt embarrassed. My mother's calls became a running joke with my friends. Also, when I wanted to stay out late with them, she would fly into a rage and accuse me of being "just like your father."

By my late teens, all I wanted to do was get away from her and my father. What I didn't know then, and do now, is that my mother tried to control me in order to counter her helplessness over control of my father's sex addiction. Of course, this only added to my confusion and sense of shame. My parents became the bookends of a story that I wanted no part of and did not ask for. They were co-conspirators in a family system that had become filled with deceit, neediness, and shame.

Just before I turned eighteen, through sheer force of will, I finally was able to leave the house. Relieved, I had hoped to put the painful legacy of my family behind me. It wasn't until my mid-to-late twenties, after a number of failed relationships, depression, addictions, and anxiety, that it became clear I hadn't. A friend, who I had also been dating, suggested it would be better to see a therapist rather than date her. It wasn't what I had in mind, but she gave me a card for a therapist, and I instinctively knew I needed to call. After I told the therapist my troubles, her first question was "Was your father an alcoholic?" I thought, *How did she know?* I am convinced that my friend and that call saved my life. It began my now lifelong journey of healing and recovery.

My first step in healing was getting therapy and support for adults who had grown up in alcoholic families. Attending groups for adults who grew up in alcoholic families was very helpful. It was there I found a home for my story. It helped tremendously to share the feelings and experiences I had long kept secret about my father's alcoholism. As much as the groups helped me, I noticed when I risked sharing about my father's sex addiction, there was little return of similar stories. I couldn't imagine I was the only one whose alcoholic parent was also a sex addict, but no one spoke of it. Once again, I felt the shame of my father's behavior as if it were mine, and I kept it secret at meetings. Fortunately, over the years, I'd had a number of good therapists and recovery friends who I was able to take those secrets to and begin to make sense of my life.

While not perfect, my life's journey began to approach "normal" as I did therapy and participated in my support groups. I learned to talk about feelings, take inventory of my family and myself, and take responsibility for my wrongs while assigning appropriate responsibility to my parents where it belonged. Slowly, I trusted others and began to want a lifelong partner. My first marriage was to a woman who had a strong religious background. She seemed like an answer to my life of carried shame. Still new in recovery, I thought little about whether we would be good friends and lovers. Our marriage was a reactive choice to my past shame rather than a clear decision about my future, and it did not last long. While regretful for my part in its development, I was grateful that I'd moved on. It was a successful and necessary divorce.

Realizing I had more work to do on myself, I dove deeper into my therapy and shared more about my experiences growing up. After an intensive therapy workshop in my early thirties, I decided to tell my mother about my father's sexual secrets that I had been carrying. The opportunity to confront my father had passed, as he had died from his alcoholism early in my healing journey before I could share the impact his sex addiction had on me. I did not want to lose the chance with my mother. Hoping to unburden myself, I gathered the courage to confront the secrets with her. When I told her, not only was she not surprised, she confessed she was aware of it all. She also revealed that she would withdraw and get depressed, in part as a way to "punish him." I was stunned. I asked if she gave any thought to my brothers and me when she did this. She looked beyond me and had little to say.

My view of my mother changed dramatically. I no longer saw her only as a victim but also as a contributor to the sick system I had grown up in. Anger replaced pity, and I began distancing myself instead of caretaking her. I also started to recognize that my excessive feelings of loyalty, guilt, and responsibility to her were a burden, and I made a decision to shed the role of her "good boy," surrogate husband, and emotional caretaker. I began to see clearly that she, too, had a negative impact on my ability to love and commit. It wasn't just my father.

Unfortunately, as I listened in my support groups, most were not speaking of the negative impact the spouse of the alcoholic had on them. Most spoke of this parent with pity. Again, I found myself having to hold back a significant aspect of my experience growing up. Instead, I took my story to my therapists and worked persistently on separating from my mother. I took more flack and criticism from her and my brothers for this than I did in confronting issues with my father. While we had all banded together over the years to complain about my father, confronting the family narrative of my mother, seen only as a victim, was not met with a similar camaraderie.

In time, I was finally able to make some peace with my mother about my experiences and feelings growing up. She also became willing to take some responsibility for her parenting missteps. In the last five years of her life, I felt free of the conflicts I'd had with her during my years growing up.

For the many years since my mother's death, I have maintained possession of her belongings in the basement of my home. Not long after her death, I found the willingness to begin sorting them out so my brothers and I could decide who received which of her keepsakes. I ran across her journal and could not help taking a look. In it, I found the testimony of her love for my father along with an assortment of love letters, some with his great regrets, to her. I was shocked; I had never seen this love between them when I was growing up, and yet there it was, clear as could be. Reading about those moments of love, I found a forgiveness for both of them that I was not expecting and didn't even realize I needed. I saw that sex addiction had robbed all of us of the love that had never left but was hidden and forgotten under the weight of betrayal, secrecy, shame, and hopelessness. It helped explain how, even after she divorced him when I was in my early twenties, she still claimed love for him and he for her. Post-divorce, I would occasionally discover them at the family home sharing a meal and talking as if that love was still there. Little did I realize their love was still there.

The growing forgiveness and healing I felt regarding my family began to take a positive hold on my life. I spent a number of years single while I worked on my issues with my mother, as well as my father, letting myself learn to date and love. My journey of being single, while certainly not perfect, opened in me the longing to settle down and have my own family. I never thought I could get there, as "family" meant "burden, pain, and betrayal." But there it was, my heart's longing for family. Soon after, I met my current wife. I knew early on she was "the one." That innocence of love I'd found earlier in my high school relationship now appeared again, this time in a new and even more exciting way. It felt like my hard-fought recovery victories were finally paying off.

We have one son, now in his late teens. My recovery lessons of open communication and dealing with problems directly have come in handy during these teen years. I am grateful, and I think he is as well. My family, and the love we share, are a gift and the result of my hard work in recovery. My son and my experiences as a father have brought a certain peace and healing from the wounds created by my father. I don't know if I can explain how, but it seems that the love I have for my son, and the connection we share, have eased the burden of sorrow left by my father. It is my greatest joy that I am able to show up as a father, enjoy my son, and pass on to him the lessons recovery has taught me.

As my own healing continues, I march forward into as many moments of love and trust as I can find the courage to enter. The support groups and therapy are sacred spaces where I heal and journey toward contentment. My parents' journey was also a testimony to the healing power of support groups. On separate occasions, and for brief lengths of time, my mother went to Al-anon and my father to Alcoholics Anonymous. I will never forget how emotionally present they seemed to me at those times. While it didn't last long for them, I won't forget the moments that were created for them, and me, as a result of their brief moments of recovery. It would have been of great help in my healing journey had there been support groups for children of sex addicts. ACSAs need their own home.

Chapter Two

Deeper Secrets: An Unwanted Legacy of Sexual Shame— Culle's Story

On Christmas Eve 1966, I received a telegram from Santa Claus. I felt excited as my father and babysitter walked me out to the mailbox for my special Christmas gift. As my little fingers tried to open the envelope and I turned seeking help from my father, I saw him kissing the babysitter. In a split second, my world went from California blue skies and puffy white clouds to black, and the stable world I knew crumbled beneath my tiny feet. I lost my breath and collapsed inside myself. When we returned to our little house, I tried to tell my mother, but as I reached out both hands to her, I didn't have the words, just sensations of distress and panic inside my little body. I was eighteen months old.

This memory surfaced around age twenty-eight, during the breakup of a relationship after learning that the man I loved and thought I was going to marry had lied, deceived, and used me from the beginning. My heart shattered into a million pieces, the same way it had after witnessing my father's infidelity. When I phoned my mother to inquire about this childhood memory, she validated the story my body had released to me. I learned for the first time that my babysitter had been her best friend, and my mother had caught my father having an affair with her. This was new information to me. Sadly, however, this was not my father's first affair. My name is Culle, and I am a recovering adult child of a sex addict.

EARLY YEARS

I spent the first seven years of my life primarily with my mother and one younger brother while my father went through medical school, residency, internship, and the service. He came and went, and I occasionally saw him at dinner or sometimes just before bed. He was tall, standing six feet, three inches, with red hair and lots of freckles. He always seemed to arrive and leave quickly and be preoccupied with something else. I look back on this time with my mother and younger brother as calm and happy. My days were filled with playing outside in the sandbox with my doll Mrs. Beasley, learning to ride my tricycle, gardening, helping my mother cook, or being curious about the different types of toys my brother played with.

When I was seven, my second brother was born, and we moved to a new city and a bigger house in the Midwest, where my father began practicing medicine as an OB-GYN. My mother got her first new car, we went out to dinner at an actual restaurant, and I got to decorate my bedroom in my favorite color, purple. For the first time, I saw my father more regularly at breakfast and dinner. I thought life was good!

In fifth grade, I received my relationship and sex talk, complete with books, pamphlets, and a box of feminine products. I recall my mother stating, "Sex is a gift and only to be shared with a man you love and who loves you in return." I went to bed that night thinking, *But that's not what you're living with Father*. My mother's description and my parents' actions were so incongruent.

One night, I was startled out of a deep sleep, hearing my parents arguing loudly and my father yelling, "You shouldn't be getting up so early to get your kids breakfast and off to school . . . you should be in bed having sex with me!" My mother was sobbing as she made her way downstairs to the extra twin bed in my youngest brother's room. This is where I joined her crying and terrified. She tried to comfort me, as I did her. I wondered, *What is sex and why is it more important than her making us breakfast and getting us off to school?* I don't recall either of my brothers waking up to the screaming and crying. I also don't recall my mother and I speaking about this again. I do know this was the second incident in my young life in which my father's rage signified that my brothers and I were not important, that we were a burden and in his way.

I remember vacation drives during my youth in which my father would pull out *Playboy* magazines from his briefcase, using the common rationalization that he "only read them for the articles." I watched as my mother's body language became rigid and angry as she drove. I was naturally curious to see what he was reading, until I saw the pictures. I felt embarrassed and confused. The atmosphere in the car, filled with my mother's unexpressed emotions and my father's shameless behavior, felt like a bomb ready to explode.

The only freedom I found as a kid was on my bicycle and on the ski slopes, with the wind and sun in my face providing breath, freedom, movement, and connection to nature and spirituality. I also experienced some shelter and privacy being alone in my room playing dress-up, experimenting with makeup and hairstyles, and listening to music and dancing.

TEEN YEARS

By the time I was an adolescent, I often heard questions like "Are you Dr. Vande Garde's daughter? Oh, he delivered my friend's baby and she loved him . . . said he was such a wonderful doctor," or "You're so lucky to have such a wonderful father . . . he delivered all my children." Although remarks like these were common about my father, I had such a different experience as his daughter. I felt a knot in the pit of my stomach that became a familiar sensation. I couldn't reconcile what others said about him versus my daily experience with him. Dr. Vande Garde was larger than life, with a lot of power as my dad, a man, and a doctor.

As an adolescent and young woman, I was innocent, naive, curious, vulnerable, embarrassed, ashamed, proud, conflicted, hurt, scared, and lonely—trying to make sense of my experiences and what others said. I had witnessed my father flirting with other women at social gatherings, heard him belittle his patients' intelligence, announce he was going drinking rather than go to a movie with his family, use slang language and derogatory words for women's body parts, and tell sexist and racist jokes at the dinner table. His behavior was rageful, self-centered, and shameless.

When I was fourteen, my father began aiming his rude comments and behavior toward me. One time, when I was lying on the floor watching sports highlights as he sat on the couch behind me, I heard him say, "You're starting to get a little too round, young lady." I felt hurt, embarrassed, and ashamed. I ran to my room, taking his words as gospel, while my mother cooked dinner out of earshot. Nothing could have been further from the truth. While I was tall and thin at five foot, eight inches, I began obsessing that I was fat. One of my worst experiences was at age sixteen. My father came home intoxicated, sought me out, and accused me of being promiscuous with a boy from my high school. Through slurred speech he said, "You have a reputation to keep up as a member of this family." I had no idea what he was talking about; I had never spent any time with this boy, and none of what he said was true. I felt hurt, shamed, and alone, with no one to talk to. A few months later I learned from my mother that, at this very time, he had been having an affair with one of his nurses. My mother had confirmed this affair by hiring a private investigator. I was shocked, devastated, and heartbroken by both his accusations and betrayal. It felt like the rug had been pulled out from under me, and I was left with no stable foundation.

As an adolescent, relationships with boys brought up fear, curiosity, excitement, vulnerability, and imperfection. For the first time I really felt myself on unequal footing with my peers. I was not as "boy crazy" as so many girls seemed to be. Today, I know this was a result of being terrified of my father and having my humanity, femininity, and sexuality shamed so severely by him. There was no safe place to be human, have crushes, be imperfect, or grow into a young woman and allow my sexuality to blossom naturally. All vulnerabilities were made fun of, put down, attacked, criticized, or shamed. I did not trust the information my mother shared with me about dating and relationships because her marriage was full of pain, betrayal, intensity, emotional, domestic, and sexual violence rather than safety, trust, comfort, connection, laughter, and love. I was very shy, self-conscious, and introverted. Looking back, I believe I protected myself by dating boys from other high schools. It was less vulnerable. Peers couldn't make fun of me, and I could learn, as I dated in private, only sharing with my two best girlfriends.

I do not recall my mother ever doing anything about my father's inappropriate behavior while growing up. Rather, I watched her quietly cook meals, assist with homework, do volunteer work, shuttle us to music lessons and sporting events, and teach us how to cook, iron our clothes, and clean our rooms. I didn't see or hear her raise her voice to him. I watched her dissociate, tolerate abusive behavior, look the other way, leave the room, cry, and take his side. In my adolescent mind, I thought she was a cook and cleaning slave with no power and no voice, trapped in a marriage with a man who treated her badly.

This created another knot inside me I could not resolve. I thought, *If that's what being a woman meant, I don't want to have anything to do with it.* I wanted to be as important as the boys or as the men who went to work and had great jobs, and who got to go out to lunch and drive new business cars. In my young eyes they were seen, heard, and valued, and were more important than women. I remember thinking to myself, *I'm as smart as the boys (if not smarter than some). I like new cars, I like to go out to lunch, and I want to have a good job. Why do they get to do and have those things, and I don't because I'm a girl? Why do I have to be stuck at home cooking and cleaning, eating leftovers, and taking care of children? My brothers know how to clean and cook.*

I wanted to be seen, heard, and valued equally as a woman, and I needed a woman's worth to be different from what I witnessed at home and in the patriarchal society I was steeped in. I wanted it to mean I could be smart, pretty, and athletic; speak the truth; be treated respectfully and with kindness; and be equal to the boys, not beneath them. I did not want to be called all the names my father called women. I didn't want my body to be degraded and objectified, be valued by my looks on a scale of 1 to 10, or be the brunt of jokes because I had blond hair.

Unfortunately, that was not the case. The only quality time my father actually spent with me growing up was when my mother was not emotionally available to him. He would then turn to me for his adult emotional needs. Initially, I felt useful, special, seen, and valued. Then, when my mother returned, he would "drop" me and stop paying me attention. I would feel depressed, lonely, and discarded. Now I realize that my father had put me in the role of the "other woman," a form of Surrogate Spouse.

YOUNG ADULT YEARS

When I was twenty, my father entered inpatient treatment for his alcoholism, and I attended my first "family week" with my mother and brothers. It was an intense and life-changing time, filled with daily lectures and assignments as well as an afternoon family group where "list work" was shared and feedback received. For the first time, I could tell the truth, my truth, about how my father's alcoholism had impacted me. It was done experientially in a safe, therapeutically guided format. He could not respond, only listen. What a relief to feel protected, guided, and to receive validating feedback from the group. I wanted and desperately needed more of this. It was as if someone had opened a door for me to take in oxygen, sunlight, and water. I could stop holding my breath and finally exhale. Telling the truth allowed me to feel hope—I felt safe and validated.

He wasn't yelling at me, making fun of me, attacking me, criticizing me, embarrassing me, or shaming me.

However, I learned something about my father that week while over-hearing a discussion between the counselors: he was a sex addict. *What was a sex addict?* That week had not included any lectures on sex addiction, book suggestions, recommended support groups, or anything about the impact of growing up with a sexually addicted parent and the roles children take on to survive sexually addicted families. I had no idea what sexual addiction was, that it was my father's primary addiction, or of its severe impact on me. I was focused on the relief I felt about him getting treatment for his alcoholism. I put the words *sex addiction* on a shelf because all I knew at that time was that he'd had an affair when I was sixteen.

When my father returned home from treatment, I experienced him as more present and somewhat anxious and unsure of himself, but kinder and less angry. He began attending support groups and weekly joint aftercare with my mother. She continued going to the support groups she'd been attending for a number of years. I took the next semester off from college to explore how I had been affected by his alcoholism and began attending my own support groups. During that semester, the relationship I was in ended, and I fell into a deep depression. As a result, I chose to enter inpatient treatment at the same treatment center my father had been in for codependence—what I now know to be childhood developmental trauma.

During my stay, I attended daily lectures on alcoholic/dysfunctional family systems and the roles children play to survive in those families, the feelings children experience, and childhood trauma. I participated in daily group therapy sessions, where I learned about self-esteem, how to identify and verbalize my emotions, give and receive feedback, and begin conceptualizing healthy boundaries. I also learned about the concept of "healthy" versus "carried" shame, attended nightly support groups, and presented homework in group sessions. I learned that, as the oldest child, I had become overly responsible and hypervigilant. I ran back and forth between my parents, emotionally stabilizing them, and was forced to look after my brothers while no one protected me. I was praised for how well I took care of everyone else, easily managed emergencies, and how "mature" I was for my age. Being told how well I did gave me a false sense of self-esteem, which reinforced the "good and perfect" persona I had adopted to survive all the responsibility placed on my young shoulders. I had no idea I'd lost myself through abandonment, enmeshment, and neglect, nor any idea of the journey I had ahead of me.

Returning home after treatment was a big adjustment. A whole new world had been opened up to me, and I felt extremely vulnerable. My college peers were not experiencing what I was. I no longer knew where I fit in. Family became a "safer" place, after four out of five family members went into treatment within a two-year period. And with each treatment came a mandatory family week. The treatment professionals applauded all the "good work" our family was doing. I attended an aftercare group once a week as well as support groups, and I had to participate in family meetings when I was home from college on the weekends. So many people told me how lucky I was to have my parents in recovery. I didn't know anything different and, looking back, I agree that I was lucky on many levels, except one. I still had no idea what sex addiction was nor its impact on me.

ADULT YEARS

My father allegedly stopped having affairs after completing his treatment; however, his objectification of women, raging, sexual/racist jokes, and boundary violations continued. For example, while driving alone with him sometime in my early thirties during a Thanksgiving holiday, he talked about his male friends in recovery who were married and had girlfriends. I sat in the passenger seat, sick to my stomach, while I got up the nerve to tell him I didn't ever want to hear about unfaithful married men who were supposedly in recovery. He said nothing and began listening to a book on CD while I held my breath in fear.

On another occasion, when I was thirty-four and visiting my parents, he came up behind me and kissed me on the neck—my mother jumped with shock, and I felt disgusted. He also patted my bottom the way he usually did to my mother, and again I felt violated. My mother would apologize for his behavior, but nothing changed. On the drive to the airport following this visit, I trembled with fear as I told him I never wanted him to stand behind me, kiss my neck, or pat my bottom again. All he said was "okay." Once I was home in Denver, it took me days to recover. I felt so ashamed and embarrassed. *Why doesn't my father know how to have an appropriate relationship with me, his daughter? Why doesn't he have healthy boundaries with me? We went to the same treatment center and had access to the same information about boundary violations!*

RECOVERY IS THE "COMMITMENT TO REALITY AT ALL COSTS"

After the relationship I was in at twenty-eight ended, I lost twenty-five pounds, stopped working in my field, waited tables for more than four years, and walked around heartbroken and depressed, a shadow of my former self. I felt so embarrassed, numb, and hollow. All of this was incongruent with what I believed about myself. I was bright, attractive, fit, honest, never used drugs, rarely drank alcohol, and had never been promiscuous. I'd earned my master's degree by age twenty-five, was in recovery from my codependence, and wanted to get married, have a couple of kids, live in Denver, and ski on the weekends—a pretty normal dream for my life.

Six months after the breakup, I began weekly therapy and figured out I had reenacted the love/avoidance addiction cycle I'd watched my parents live. This cycle was based on betrayal, not trust. During therapy, my body continued to release repressed memories to me that my mother again validated. It turns out the first time my father had been unfaithful was when my mother was pregnant with me, and she chose to stay married despite his infidelity. It didn't take me long to start asking myself what relationships based on safety and trust looked and felt like. I traced the pattern of abandonment and betrayal in friendships and romantic relationships back to middle school. I now wanted all my relationships with women and men to be based on safety and trust rather than disloyalty. With a lot of therapy, self-help books, and support groups, I stopped putting the needs and wants of others over my own. I found the courage to date again and was blessed with two very healing, romantic relationships, which showed me the kind of safety and trust I'd been looking for.

Over the years, I completed three family-of-origin intensives to release all the shame, pain, fear, and anger I carried from my parents. I've made at least ten different affirmation recordings in my own voice, and listened to them while exercising to connect with my inherent value and equality as a person and woman. By listening to the recordings, I unknowingly began re-parenting all the wounded, reactive, and controlling parts of myself. Having inherent worth, simply because I was born and believed I was a child of God, became my new foundation and the beginning of my own value system. I then learned to protect and contain my body, thoughts, feelings, and behavior with healthy boundary systems. I learned I had a lot of distorted beliefs and stories I had created based on the extremes of my childhood experiences, so I had the opportunity to learn how to restructure these cognitive distortions and create a more kind, compassionate, loving dialogue with myself and others. I journaled my emotions daily and paid attention to the sensations I felt within my body, which also assisted me in self-care and living within my values. I exercised, ate healthy, and began working in my field again. I learned the difference between my needs and my wants, and how to hold people in "warm positive regard" when their thoughts, feelings, and behaviors were different from my own. I explored, embraced, and redefined my femininity, sexuality, and womanhood for myself. I learned how to embrace my imperfection and humanity as the "norm" and to live a lot more moderately. All the internal work I did on restructuring my relationship with myself subsequently changed the type of friendships and romantic relationships I have in my life today.

MAKING PEACE WITH MY PAST

It has taken me the better part of thirty years to piece my story together. Sexual-addiction treatment was in its infancy in 1985 when my father went to treatment. I do not know what support groups or therapy were available or recommended at that time. And to my knowledge, only one book had been published about sexual addiction in the early 1980s. I really needed the same family-week process I had experienced previously but with education on sex addiction and the roles children adopt to survive the sexually addicted family. I also needed an opportunity to share the impact both my parents' behavior had on me, set boundaries, and hear them take responsibility for their individual and collective behaviors, commit to their own recoveries, and make amends. I also needed support groups focused on healing and recovery as an ACSA. Finally, I had needed skilled therapists who were clinically trained in treating ACSAs, and who knew and understood the impact of growing up in a sexually addicted family—the characteristics, roles, and healing journey.

I've had to accept a lot of facts and grieve a lot of losses to make peace with my story, my parents' choices, their trauma histories, and the legacies handed down to them. I had to forgive my parents for their behavior, forgive society's messages and the lack of treatment for sexual addiction, and embrace the belief that "I cannot make the past different, better, or more." I had to forgive myself for what I didn't know and for what my own behavior cost me. I am so grateful for my relationship with my higher power, Mother Nature and her daily changes through the four seasons, along with the numerous men and women who have crossed my path and assisted me on my healing path to myself. I learned that nothing on my journey was ever wasted, every part has had its purpose. I'm so grateful for the spiritual family I have today that is made up of loving friends and extended family. My hope is that by sharing my story and writing this book, ACSAs can find the courage, love, and support needed to heal the impact of growing up in a sexually addicted family.

Chapter Three

Lost in the Storm of an Addicted Legacy— Mary's Story

My name is Mary, and I am an adult child of a sex addict. This is the story of my experiences growing up with a sexually addicted parent and the impact it had on me. I was born into the middle of a raging storm of addiction and trauma that had been going on for generations. I didn't understand this as a child, and I blamed myself for my confusion and struggle. I denied my feelings, and I thought it was my job to protect my parents from their own issues. I thought there was something wrong with me at times, and I hated my body, my femininity, and my powerlessness. I felt shame and fear so often that it became the baseline of my daily life. I struggled with anxiety and depression as a child, and I retreated into perfectionism and fantasy to escape the painful reality of my family situation. I've struggled to understand the story of my childhood for many years. I longed for something that would help me dig my way up, out of the hole in my heart.

After struggling with the impact of sex addiction on my family through-out my life, trying to understand it, and asking my higher power for help, I began a path of recovery that continues today. Now, I have hope for the future, I practice being present, and I strive toward healthy intimacy. My recovery is cyclical—with each step forward, I grieve another piece of the past. Acknowledging the reality of my history and feeling the grief allows me to move through it bit by bit, freeing myself from the painful legacy that used to hold me hostage.

I used to think I was alone in my struggles. I didn't know anyone else who had been through the things I had. Now I know that isn't true. There are so many people who have suffered from the effects of a parent's sex addiction, without help or even the awareness or language to ask for it. Perhaps ACSAs will see something in my story that helps them make sense of their own, so that they too can find their voices.

When my mother was seven months pregnant with me, my parents had an intense argument about my father's infidelity. My mother told me it was the worst they had ever had. I can imagine the fear, rage, and adrenaline that went coursing through her body as she felt the wounds of betrayal. They also went coursing through my body. When I was born, my father may have been having an affair with the woman who lived down the street, with someone at the local liquor store, or maybe both. My parents' marriage had already been riddled with the effects of sex addiction for years before I, their first child, arrived. I was formed inside the body of a woman who felt chronic stress from intimate betrayal and was fathered by the man who betrayed her. The shadow of trauma and addiction that had been part of my family for generations was now mine.

As a young child, I remember my parents fighting often, but I had no awareness of what the fights were about. I just stayed out of the way. They were the anchors to my world, like the ground beneath me, as I began to learn and grow. Although I felt much safer with my mother, I reveled in the moments I had my father's attention—driving in the car with him, listening to music, or building a snow fort outside. I longed for his time and attention, even though I also shied away from his chronic irritability.

When I was seven years old, I learned my parents were divorcing, and my world came crashing down around me. The months that followed this announcement were devastating to me. My father moved into our basement, and my parents' arguing escalated dramatically, focusing mainly on my father's infidelities, drinking, and unexplained absences. My already emotionally distant father became almost nonexistent. My younger brother and I found ourselves in the crosshairs as my parents waged war on each other. For the first time, I felt my body tense up in fear and dread; stress took up residence in my muscles and remained there, even when things were calm. My heart would beat fast, and I would tingle with adrenaline, making me jumpy and on alert. I began feeling sick to my stomach regularly, as if a dark pit now resided where my insides used to be. It was not until well into my recovery as an adult that I could finally name that sick feeling as "carried" shame and fear.

My first "disclosure" took place soon after my parents separated. My mother had me read a note she had discovered in my father's belongings that he had written to one of his affair partners. She told me she wanted me to see it, so I would know the divorce was not what she wanted—it was my father's fault. I remember vividly the profound and irreversible shift that took place inside me, from my carefree innocence as a child to the heavy burden of adult problems I had no business knowing. I had many other, staggered disclosures of my father's betrayals in the coming months and years, all devastating, but this first one hit me the hardest. I was overwhelmed with the information and by my mother's pain and anger. I did not have the ability to process my own, let alone hers.

My parents fought viciously with each other during their separation process and in the years following their divorce. There were some arguments that became violent, which my little brother and I were present for. At these times, I was unable to move, feeling frozen and numb. My brother cried in terror, but I felt nothing. I recall secret missions with my mother in the middle of the night to find out where my father was, which was confusing to me because it was exciting and devastating at the same time. Once, my mother told me to retrieve the liquor bottles and pornography from the back of my father's car after one of his nights out. I followed my mother's instructions and took them to my father, asleep in the basement. When I woke him to give him the items, fear, confusion, and shame raced through my body. I felt wholly responsible for everything as if I were the one who had done something wrong. I was an innocent little girl trapped in between my parents who seemed unaware of the impact their actions were having on me.

My family was dissolving in front of my eyes, and there was nothing I could do to change its course. I felt devastated and powerless. But my mother praised me for being strong and "wise beyond my years," and I felt proud and falsely empowered. From then on, I tried to be strong for my mother as she struggled with the impact of my father's betrayals, now as a single, working mother raising two children on her own. She confided to me her sadness, struggles, and resentments. I did not understand then how damaging this "adult information" was for me to hold, or how confused I had become about my role in our family. I did what I could to be helpful and pretend that I didn't have the hurricane of feelings circling inside me. I focused on being perfect in school and making no waves at home. I was not "okay," but I did my best to pretend that I was, so I could regain some sense of safety and control over my life.

As I became a teen, I felt pressured further into an adult role before I was ready, being expected to keep up with housework, keep track of my brother after school, and take on responsibilities that would otherwise have been an adult's had there been a second one in the house. My mother resented having to do everything on her own, and she often took her frustration out on my brother and me. I resented this and felt unseen and unheard by her. My sense of shame grew for not being able to make her happy. I needed her to attune to *my* needs, help me learn about safety and trust in relationships, and gently guide me into womanhood, but she was still preoccupied in her own struggles. Caretaking, abandoning my own needs for others, and "doing it all myself" became entrenched patterns that I continued to enact as an adult.

My father offered very little by way of explanation to me about his departure from my life. Truthfully, he was emotionally absent from my life long before he physically left. He spoke to me only once about his leaving, the night before he moved out. He asked me if I would still love him if he lived somewhere else. I immediately felt caught and hesitated with my answer. Of course, I loved him—all I wanted was for him to be happy so that he would stay and we could still be a family. I thought of saying "no" so he might rethink his plans for leaving us, but already desperate for his love and approval, I told him, "yes," I would still love him. He tucked me in and kissed me good night for the last time and left. I immediately began beating myself up about this, fixating on the possibility of changing his mind had I answered differently. By asking me for my permission to leave, he was acting shamelessly, not taking full responsibility for his decision and subtly asking me to help carry his burden. This interaction with him, and others like it, would set me up for years of distorted thinking, emotional turmoil, and codependency in my future relationships with men. It began a pattern of denying my own needs, taking on too much responsibility, blaming myself for others' actions, feeling "not quite worthy enough" of others' love, and putting up with intolerable behavior in an effort to not be abandoned. Love and pain became twisted together, grotesque and beautiful to me at the same time.

My father moved in with my future stepmother and her daughters very soon after he left our house for good. I felt abandoned by him and replaced by his "new family." I would often cry at night, unable to sleep. I wondered, *Why am I not important enough for him to stay and be my dad?* The shame and pain I felt became lodged inside me physically, making my body an uncomfortable place to inhabit. I gained weight. I often stayed home sick from school, confusing the sick feeling of fear and shame in my stomach for physical illness. I became shy and withdrawn. I would have shame attacks when the teacher would call on me at school—my eyes watering and my skin becoming hot as I struggled to force out sound. I began living in my own inner world, retreating into fantasy about relationships with boys and focusing on creating a perfect family of my own as soon as possible, instead of enjoying my childhood. I didn't understand that these were the effects of my unresolved trauma.

One evening when I was twelve, my father took my brother and me with him to spend the night at an affair partner's house after an argument with my stepmother. I asked to be taken home to my mother's house, but he refused. So, I lay awake in an unfamiliar house that night as strangers came and went past my bedroom door. I was scared and angry, and I prayed morning would come quickly without incident. In the morning, my father asked me not to tell anyone where we had been. I felt angry and sick to my stomach, but all I could do was sit silently and wait to be taken home. I remember making a note to myself then, "I will never depend on a man when I grow up—they can't be trusted."

I often felt unsafe when visiting my father. Repeatedly, I would ask to leave situations in which I was uncomfortable, but each time I was ignored and disregarded. When I asked to go home, he would become angry and yell, "You are *my* child, and I have the *right* to see you when I want!" Eventually, I stopped asking. I learned to "manage" even the most unmanageable of situations by suppressing and controlling my emotions. My face would look calm in any storm, I decided, even if it was raging on the inside. My father was only concerned with his own wants and needs. He left me chronically unprotected, vulnerable, and scared. His lack of supervision, emotional neglect, and preoccupation with himself resulted in me learning to tolerate unsafe situations and people, to act against my own impulse to protect myself as a means of survival, and to remain silent for years when I was being abused by others.

Then, when I was fourteen years old, my father abruptly dropped out of contact with me. My half-sister had recently been born, and I had been feeling at peace with my family situation. It hit me like a punch in the gut when, for the second time in my life, my family disintegrated before my eyes. My father had gotten into legal trouble for inappropriate sexual behavior at work. My stepmother decided to divorce him, and he attempted suicide. I felt betrayal on many levels, but I did not have the capacity to understand or express these feelings yet. I had just experienced a second big disclosure of my father's sex addiction, news about the implosion of part of my family as well as the graphic details of my father's attempt to end his life. I felt confused, angry, grief-stricken, but mostly numb. I felt humiliated and ashamed when I discovered my father's name and picture could be found on the state sex offender registry with a simple internet search. I grieved the loss of my stepsisters and half-sister, with whom I had grown close, but I no longer saw, and remained unaware of where my father went or what happened to him. I was almost sixteen years old when my father resurfaced, briefly, providing little explanation for his absence. I didn't ask—I wanted him to believe that I was unaffected by his betrayal and abandonment. But no matter how much I tried not to be affected, on the inside my invisible wounds ripped back open every time we spoke, and I hurt deeply.

I have had limited contact with my father as an adult. When I was in my early twenties, I confronted him about his past infidelities that had destroyed my family. He denied having ever been unfaithful at all to my mother or stepmother and instead painted a picture of himself as a victim. He lied to me unapologetically and attempted to convince me that my own memories were untrue. I was angry and hurt that he refused to hear me. I questioned my own sanity and perceptions, even though I knew what my truth was. I felt silenced by his lies and manipulation. I didn't know the word *gaslighting* then, but I experienced the way it made me feel powerless and crazy.

Throughout these young adult years, my ability to be in healthy, loving connections with other people suffered. Only looking back can I see that I was playing out the same painful scenario over and over, in which I formed relationships with people despite feeling used, abandoned, or emotionally cut off from them. My internal belief was that I had to accept manipulation and betrayal in a relationship if I wanted to be loved. I was attracted to people who were also unable to be in emotionally healthy relationships. Many of my friendships ended with me feeling betrayed and abandoned. I struggled with deep insecurity in my relationships with men. I was often fearful that my partner was going to leave me for other women or that he was keeping secrets from me. I remained in a relationship when I was betrayed by my partner's sexual behavior, and my boundaries were broken repeatedly. I believed if I were just more attractive or interesting or just better in some unknown way, I would be worthy of my partner's loyalty and faithfulness. His lack thereof felt sadly normal and familiar to me. The festering wounds left by my father's betrayals and abandonment had seeped into my mind and infected my choices in romantic relationships.

My attempts to cope with the effects of sex addiction led me into many behaviors as an adult that were not in my best interest. I continued to be controlled by fear and shame in my daily life, remaining quiet and withdrawn when any perceived emotional threat surfaced. I struggled with my body image, my femininity, and my sexuality. I learned that being a woman in my family meant being used and devalued. I learned to be at war with my body, thinking it was never "good enough." I also learned that sex is dangerous—it has the ability to destroy families and take everything I value in life away from me. So, I shut myself off to healthy, authentic sexuality for many years and used it only as a tool to secure romantic relationships. I have over-functioned in work and home life, consistently taking on more than my share of responsibility and overworking to exhaustion. I tried to "manage" everything, grasping at control, determined to make things work out, even if it meant sacrificing myself. I have betrayed myself consistently for the illusion of emotional safety. My unwillingness to be moderately vulnerable has cut me off from healthy intimacy in many of my relationships and fueled the chronic feeling of loneliness and not belonging anywhere. Even as an adult, I feared my parents' emotions and disapproval, despite being able to function well emotionally in other areas of my life. The most devastating loss I suffered has been the ability to speak my truth—I have struggled to have a voice and a story of my own.

In my late twenties I learned the term *sex addiction*. When I discovered this, I was finally able to make sense of the complicated story of my childhood. I was finally able to put words to my confusing experiences, and I realized I wasn't the only one who carried these kinds of wounds from childhood. It was a relief, but it was only the very beginning of my recovery journey. Now, I practice being in recovery as an adult child of a sex addict. This means that I work toward living in *my* truth, not someone else's. I practice integrity with my values, and I set boundaries to protect myself. I work hard at assigning appropriate responsibility instead of carrying around shame and guilt that does not belong to me, and I parent myself gently and lovingly, with limits and protection. I look to my higher power for guidance in my daily life. I have worked with therapists and other helpers and healers over many years to heal from the effects of sex addiction. I have a daily meditation practice and a relationship with a higher power that I credit with my ability to tolerate the pain of healing, integration, and transformation. I have also been involved in various support groups that have helped me greatly, and I have found a spiritual community that is nourishing to my heart and soul. I have found that recovery remains a daily choice, a spiritual practice, and a continually evolving journey.

I understand now that I was not responsible for my parents or any of the pain that they were in. I do not have to continue feeling shame or a sense of responsibility for other people's pain or how they act that pain out. It is not my fault, and it is not my job to make it better. It is my job to take care of myself and to cultivate a healthier value system around responsibility, self-worth, and relationships. I try to take what I've learned about surviving the effects of sex addiction in my family of origin and transform them into something useful to others. This is the motivation and passion for my work as a licensed marital and family therapist. I try to use the energy from my own healing process to inspire and facilitate change in other families who have similarly been devastated by sex addiction.

My father is not in recovery and is still in deep denial about his illness and the devastation it has caused him and our entire family. I have accepted that he may never choose recovery for himself and that I may never find the relational healing with him that I wish for. I love my father, and there is a part of me who may always long for "the relationship that never was" with him. But I can accept things as they are, and I can accept him as he is. The reality is I get to choose recovery only for myself. I believe, as an ACSA, that I have the right to request a formal disclosure from my father, for him to take responsibility for the hurt he has caused, and for him to hear how his behavior has impacted me. I also accept that this will probably not happen, and I will find my healing and recovery with others who are able and willing to choose emotional honesty and accountability. It has been one of the most painful lessons of my life to learn that I can love someone, but I cannot change them, and that my only responsibility is to myself. I choose for myself a legacy of compassion, honesty, integrity, and freedom. I choose to give my children a different life than I had—they will learn that they deserve love and respect, that they are protected and safe, and that their voices matter. I will do all I can to make sure they do not have to cope with addiction, abandonment, emotional neglect, or abuse. They will learn how to value themselves because they will grow up watching me learning to value myself.

Despite the difficulties I have experienced in my childhood, I have been blessed ten-fold with many loving and supportive relationships, which have allowed me to be a functional adult today. I've received so much help from my higher power—with moments of clarity, messages received just in time, helpers and friends to guide me, and waking up every day with breath still in my lungs. I believe that all my experiences have been a gift, even if unwrapping them has been difficult. I am grateful to my ancestors who I know struggled to heal parts of this legacy while they were alive, passing on what blessings they could. I am grateful to my parents for giving me what they had to give of themselves. In the end it was enough—here I am alive on this planet, doing the work I was meant to do, living a happy, fulfilling life. Without the challenges I faced so early in my life, I would not have had the opportunity to become the resilient, tenacious, passionate woman I am proud to be today.

I hope by telling my story, I can inspire other ACSAs who still suffer to find their voices. I believe by telling our stories as adult children of sex addicts, we can be a light shining in the dark—our own anchor to safety in the storm of the sex addiction that we found ourselves in as children and aspire to rebuild from as adults. For me, the struggle of growing up in the wake of devastation from sex addiction was immense, but I have learned that it cannot keep me from wholeness, joy, my ability to be in connection with others, or my relationship with my Higher Power. I was wounded by that storm, but I have weathered it, and I am safe now. I didn't choose the beginning, but I *will* choose how my story ends—free to be my truest self and with a full and peaceful heart.

Chapter Four

The Characteristics

While each ACSA has a unique story, many share a common set of experiences. The following characteristics have emerged from our observations:

1. ACSAs carry shame about their sexuality and are often confused about appropriate sexual behavior for others and themselves.

Having witnessed or been aware of a parent's sexual addiction, ACSAs may find their own sexuality a battleground. Living in a family that oversexualizes many interactions—such as sexual joking, inappropriate nudity, sexual remarks about bodies and gender, knowledge of a parent's affairs, and other hypersexualized experiences—leaves children curious and ashamed, and later confused about appropriate sexual expression. Similar confusion may also emerge when the sexually addicted family hides the inappropriate behaviors in the home through public overmoralizing and shaming of natural sexual expression. Either the addict or the spouse, or both, can do this moralizing. The addict and his or her partner thus transfer their shame to the child, who absorbs the transferred shame as their own and experiences a conflicted sexuality. As adults, they may be hypersexual, sexually avoidant, emotionally shut down, and/or judgmental and controlling regarding their own and others' sexuality.

2. **ACSAs are often uncomfortable with their bodies and gender and may go to extremes to compensate. They might purposely make themselves unattractive to others or overvalue being attractive.**

This happens as a result of the child directly observing two extremes in both the addict and the addict's partner. On one hand, the child may witness a parent oversexualizing. Some examples are prolonged, intrusive sexual looking at others, extreme emphasis on the physical attributes of either gender, verbalizing inappropriate sexual comments about another's body or gender, touching or hugging others without consent, dressing provocatively, obsessive preoccupation with how they look or how their partner looks, working out to the extreme, or a parent's chronic flirting or sexual activities outside the marriage.

On the other hand, the child also may notice a parent becoming hypervigilant and/or shut down. Some examples are preoccupation with the other partner, excessive crying, depression, inability to get out of bed, dressing down in clothing that covers their body, hiding their sexuality, excessive anxiety, overemphasizing church or God, reacting to sexuality in the media, excessive interest in who their child is dating, or no interest at all.

As a result, the child internalizes the messages that their appearance, body, or gender are more important than who they are as a human being. This creates a belief system that relationships and love are based on a distorted or skewed currency rather than on safety, trust, and authenticity. Alternatively, some children avoid or minimize their bodies, appearance, or gender in an effort to protect against unwanted attention that feels intrusive, objectified, or sexualized. They do not learn to hold their bodies or gender with esteem or value. In both extremes, ACSAs are unable to create a healthy relationship with their bodies and who they are as women or men. Nonbinary people and LGBTQ+ individuals may have had a related but different experience and will need to sort this characteristic as it relates to their own unique circumstances. For example, they may carry extra shame from being criticized or bullied due to displaying nontraditional or non-heteronormative gender roles as children.

3. ACSAs can either be uncomfortable with physical touch or feel an insatiable need for it.

Physical touch takes on a different meaning for ACSAs than it does for others. The sexually addicted parent may have crossed boundaries with the child, or the child may have witnessed the parent using touch to cross other people's boundaries. Sometimes the nonaddicted parent uses physical closeness to meet adult needs that the marriage is not providing. In these instances, touch becomes shaming and intrusive. The ACSA continues to distrust touch in adult life, avoiding it because it hurts or creates a fear of being engulfed.

Conversely, healthy physical touch may be missing or withheld completely, due to both parents being preoccupied and consumed by the sexual addiction itself or because the parent(s) are unavailable emotionally. The child's needs for physical love and affection are neglected, and an insatiable longing for physical closeness and touch is taken into adult relationships. In both instances, the healthy, nurturing intimacy that should accompany physical touch in relationships is not achieved.

4. ACSAs can be extreme in their sexual attitudes—either too permissive or too judgmental.

ACSAs may be unable to develop a healthy approach to sexuality in adult life because they learned sex is either out in the open (overly talked about and displayed shamelessly with no boundaries) or is a secret (something to be ashamed of, dirty or bad, with rigid, moral rules and severe consequences). For example, when the addict makes sexual jokes at the nightly dinner table and their partner remains silent yet is visibly embarrassed and ashamed, the children are all impacted emotionally, intellectually, physically, sexually, and spiritually. At the same time, when a child innocently stumbles upon the addict's pornography stash and starts watching it on the family big-screen TV, and the Mom walks in, the child experiences her mom's uncontained rage and extreme punishment for being curious about what she had found. Thus, the child may receive mixed messages about sex and sexuality from both parents, leaving them feeling confused, anxious, shamed, and lonely.

Sadly, this is common for ACSAs, leading them to experience unbalanced thoughts about sex and sexuality and leaving them on their own to figure it out. Often, they find themselves doing and saying the same things they witnessed in their turbulent family environment.

5. ACSAs can become sexually compulsive or sexually avoidant, either sexualizing experiences not meant to be sexual or retreating and escaping when it is actually safe and healthy to be sexual.

ACSAs' relationships with their own sexuality has been unknowingly affected by the confusing sexual dynamics created by their parents. Some learn the skewed belief that they need sex in order to be happy and fulfilled, chasing after it relentlessly. On the other extreme, some ACSAs learn to ignore and avoid intimate relationships in which sex is a healthy and safe option. Unconsciously, they are afraid of it, believing that avoiding sex will protect them from being hurt, made fun of, shamed, betrayed, or taken advantage of. For example, an everyday interaction in life such as "Hello, nice to see you" is interpreted as "I want to have sex with you." One ACSA will hear this and pursue the potential to be sexual while another will interpret it as a threat and hide behind walls to avoid any possibility of exploring sexuality. In both extremes, ACSAs may interpret signals incorrectly and may not be able to discover the gifts of their own sexuality.

6. ACSAs often view someone's sexual interest as a sign of love or as a violation, although neither one may be accurate.

Growing up in sexually addicted family systems, some children learn to equate sex with love while others equate it with danger and fear. They grow up witnessing the addicted parent lie—using betrayal, gaslighting, and sexual abuse as a commodity or replacement for genuine intimacy in their relationship. They also watch the other parent tolerate shameless behavior and loss of self while making an effort to cope as the foundation of the partnership unravels. The betrayed partner's actions often turn into obsession, manipulation, anxiety, preoccupation with the addict's behavior, excessive need for control, depression, and/or their own addictions. As a result, ACSAs tend to misread others' intentions, filtering them through the distorted lenses they learned in childhood. For example, when a romantic interest asks to have a first kiss, one ACSA may accept, believing that the kiss means that they are now in a committed love relationship while another ACSA experiences a fear response, loss of boundaries, and is unable to decline.

7. ACSAs can be drawn to and overvalue the intensity, risk, drama, and sexual excitement in an intimate relationship.

In their families of origin, children of sex addicts are immersed in the emotional intensity of their parents' toxic cycle of interaction. Sex is the primary focus of the addicted parent while grief, loss, confusion, and preoccupation become the norm for the partner. As a result, the children's needs become secondary. In order for them to try to meet their own needs, they mistake the learned intensity for intimacy. They carry the confused and distorted belief systems into adulthood, often reenacting the unconscious patterns or roles from their relationships with either parent.

Consequently, ACSAs cultivate risk and drama by crossing boundaries and going against value systems, fueling sexual excitement and intensity rather than authentic, respectful sharing and connection. They may ask, "When did my life become such a reality show?" ACSAs are used to a steady diet of intensity from their families of origin, and the crossing of boundaries feels normal because that was required of them as children.

8. ACSAs unknowingly lack healthy value systems and sexual boundaries.

Due to their parents' toxic addiction cycle, children of sex addicts often grow up not knowing about healthy sexual boundaries or value systems. While many parents verbally espouse values like honesty, integrity, safety, and body respect, their behaviors display the opposite. Children often experience their own boundaries being violated and/or devalued by either or both parents. This creates the internal experience of feeling defective, less than, or not mattering. It sets the stage for using defense mechanisms that under- or overprotect them from this toxic feeling of shame.

As adults, ACSAs may continue to act without regard to their own safety and well-being, looking to others' wants and needs to determine their own behavior. Having no internal emotional anchors to keep them from drifting off their desired course, they are vulnerable in relationships. Many also choose partners who reenact the dysfunctional dynamics witnessed in both their families of origin. This is seen in the couple who argues about pornography. One partner dislikes the other using it and lacks the ability to communicate their displeasure or set limits. Simultaneously, the other partner fails to see the negative impact their behavior is having on their partner and is unable to empathize with the other's pain.

9. ACSAs are either hypervigilant or unaware of the role of safety, trust, and play in relationships.

Children from sexually addicted families may have no firsthand experience with authentic safety and trust relationally. They only know dishonesty, betrayal, secrets, exploitation, and lies as the norm. Hypervigilance and avoidance become the two primary coping strategies used to keep themselves "safe" from the unreliable behavior of both major caregivers.

Hypervigilant children experience abandonment in their relationships with their moms or dads or both. This comes across as anxiety and preoccupation, and their internal dialogue becomes *Please don't leave me! Please don't leave me!* They become extremely skilled at using their five senses to "read" their parents or a situation and turn into who they think their mom or dad needs them to be. For example, they master listening to tones of voice, watch facial expressions, are sensitive to cold and heat on their skin or face, and often sense what others are feeling.

On the other hand, avoidant children of sex addicts are managing overwhelming feelings of suffocation and intensity due to being enmeshed by one or both parents. Their behavior comes across as distancing and escaping, and their internal dialogue becomes *Please don't hurt me! Please don't hurt me!* They become extremely skilled at using avoidance strategies to stop feeling consumed emotionally. From both situations, the ACSAs are adapting to and surviving the instability of the sexually addicted family system. These two coping methods become the foundation of ACSAs' relationship patterns.

10. ACSAs may overcommit and try to fix those who have hurt them emotionally and/or sexually.

As children, ACSAs can experience emotional, intellectual, physical, sexual, and spiritual abuse, both overtly and covertly. Types of abuse include abandonment, betrayal, enmeshment, exploitation, neglect, rage, shaming, silence, unwarranted accusations, innuendos, and secret keeping. Children have no knowledge that their parents' behaviors are shameless and abusive. Being dependent as children, they also have no choice but to conform to their parents' neediness and expectations. Children are "rewarded" with praise for being "Mom's good boy" or "Dad's confidante." This gives the child a false sense of self-esteem and sadly becomes one of the primary ways they feel validated and loved. However, in reality the child is being forced to betray themselves. This betrayal becomes an unconscious foundational pattern of "giving themselves away" in order to be loved and shows itself by overcommitting, overfunctioning, "fixing," or "helping" others. ACSAs are looking for self-esteem, validation, and love outside themselves. They can trace this pattern back through their childhood friendships, teenage romances, adult work associations, parental relationships, and romantic partnerships.

11. ACSAs may have difficulty sharing their vulnerability and trusting in intimate relationships.

ACSAs often have trouble creating, establishing, and committing to intimate relationships. For an ACSA, relationships trigger a minefield of unresolved feelings of confusion, fear, pain, loneliness, anger, and carried shame from their childhood wounds of abandonment, enmeshment, and neglect. The history of being left alone, chronically betrayed, and unprotected is the foundation from which ACSAs attempt to create relationships. Consequently, they are consciously or unconsciously drawn to friendships and partnerships that reenact their family of origin dynamics and roles, simply because it is all they know. They live with an internal competition between the natural human desire for closeness and connection and the need for self-protection from further hurt and violation from someone they "love" and depend on. As a result of this wounding, trust has always been in question for adult children of sex addicts. It has been absent, betrayed, broken, ruptured, and violated.

12. ACSAs often continue to declare loyalties to their families of origin by allowing themselves to be used by their parents for comfort, to combat loneliness, or to stabilize them emotionally at a high cost to themselves, their intimate partnership, relationships with children, and family of choice.

ACSAs find it difficult to stop feeling obligated to emotionally "caretake" their parents, having been conditioned to do this in childhood. For example, a child may have found themself in the role of "Mom's lookout partner"—brought along at night to see if Dad's car is parked at his affair partner's home. Or, as a child, another ACSA may have become his mother's dinner companion every Friday night to comfort her while her husband is "working late." Still another ACSA may have found herself reassuring her sexually addicted father that his infidelity "wasn't that bad." These children feel confused, hurt, and resentful about this role reversal without understanding why. Their declaration of loyalty is misguided and is never a child's job. However, children don't know that and will do whatever "helps" the intense emotions and conflict dissipate at that time. This maladaptive coping skill makes children feel a false sense of safety, esteem, and value and, when left unchallenged, creates long-lasting patterns into adulthood.

ACSAs can feel used, depleted, and trapped in these destructive childhood patterns, not knowing how to change their roles without feeling intense shame and guilt. They may continue to declare loyalties to their families of origin and enter their parents' or siblings' conflicts, left over from the betrayal, to fix and repair the damage caused by sexual addiction. They are compelled to pick sides and

Chapter Five

The Moral Hero and Champion

ichael, the head pastor in a large church, found himself mandated to individual therapy by the Christian General Council after being disciplined for "inappropriate relationships" with women in his congregation. He had been suspended from his post after multiple women came forward claiming "uncomfortable sexual commentary" and "sexual touching and groping" while alone with Michael. During his initial therapy session, Michael tearfully lamented, *I don't know how I got here. I've always prided myself on being a godly man. This isn't who I am.*

At age forty-two, Michael and his wife, Sarah, had been the faces of a large Christian church for the past twelve years. They'd married right after college, and both saw their purpose in life as "service to others." Michael started his career as a youth minister while insisting Sarah stay home with their growing family. He had very rigid ideas about the roles men and women should play. It was important to him that Sarah stay at home, care for their children, and attend church activities dutifully, just as his own mother had done in his childhood. Michael was charismatic and a dynamic speaker who commanded attention. By the time he was thirty, he had been promoted to senior pastor and head of religious services in his region.

Michael espoused high moral standards. He preached passionately on Sundays about the importance of "being of service to others," traditional family values, and living within "biblical principles." Michael had recently published his first book, *Head of the House: A Biblical Guide to Manhood*. He felt strongly about the importance of men's roles in the family as his own father had abandoned him and his mother to live with his latest affair partner when Michael was twelve. Michael also harshly criticized the use of pornography. No one knew that he had been struggling with pornography use off and on himself since adolescence. What began as healthy exploration soon turned into a coping strategy to manage overwhelming emotions during times of stress. It was an easy escape from the pressure he felt to always be perfect for his family and congregation.

Early in their marriage, Sarah had stumbled upon a pornographic image on Michael's computer. He had repented and promised her it would never happen again. Sarah took him at his word. From then on he presented himself as a devoted husband, father, and dedicated servant who wanted to bring out the best in people. He felt deeply conflicted about his compulsive use of pornography but found himself going back to it again and again. Michael appeared to have everything anyone could want—a beautiful wife, loving children, a big home, and a fulfilling career. Nevertheless, he felt alone and sad much of the time, and he outwardly went to extreme lengths to project a well-constructed persona.

Sarah felt extremely proud of her husband for having such devotion to helping people who were struggling and for being a good role model to their own young children. She reminded herself of this when Michael was working long hours at the church, counseling women on the weekends, and even helping single moms with handiwork in their homes. She was blindsided by the allegations! The man she knew lived his life according to their shared morals and values. She couldn't believe it was true. After all, Michael was usually not interested in sex with her and was never one to flirt or be affectionate. It didn't make sense he would be flirting with other women and unfaithful to her. The contradictions were too great for her to understand.

In therapy, as Michael began exploring his family of origin, he began to make connections between his current situation and growing up with a sexually addicted father. Michael recounted his parents' constant arguing about his father "not being a good man" and how his mother would spend hours on the phone seeking emotional support and comfort from the family's pastor. Soon after Michael turned twelve, his dad moved his belongings out of the house and never came home again. The only explanation Michael's mom gave him was "Your dad has a girlfriend."

During middle school, Michael learned his dad had been chronically unfaithful. He felt tremendously hurt, embarrassed, and betrayed by his father's behavior. Late at night, shedding silent tears, Michael would wonder, *Why did you do this to us? Weren't we good enough for you?*

Why don't you love us anymore? He began promising himself he would never be like his father; he would be a much better husband and father to his own family someday. He also adopted his mother's religiosity as a way to connect with her and distance himself from being anything like his father. He began paying close attention in Sunday school so he could learn how to be a "good person." When he overheard a teacher tell his mother what a caring and thoughtful boy he was, he felt relieved that she liked him. On the inside, he beamed with pride, thinking he was better than his father.

Throughout high school and college, Michael had very little contact with his father. Over the following years, his pain and shame turned into judgment and disgust. He set out to become the man his father never was, dedicating himself to religious service. With the help of his therapist, he began to see how so much of his time and energy had been put into trying to be the perfect husband, father, and pastor in order to make up for his father's shameless sexual behavior. Michael's recovery from the role of Moral Hero and Champion required the following: taking responsibility for his inappropriate sexual behavior with women, accepting and understanding his humanity and imperfection, unburdening feelings of carried shame and pain from childhood, resigning from overresponsibility and being the "expert," creating a support system in which he could ask for help and be accountable to other men in recovery, and learning the relational skills necessary to rebuild his marriage.

DESCRIPTION AND CHARACTERISTICS OF THE MORAL HERO AND CHAMPION

Sex addiction leaves children ashamed and confused about what is normal sexual behavior. They often hide from others the painful and shameful reality caused by the addict's behavior. Often, this "carried" shame is hidden from public view, but it's internalized by the children as their burden. In an attempt to counter the shamefulness caused by sex addiction, the Moral Hero and Champion of the family either takes it upon himself or is given the distinct message by one of the parents to show the outside world that their family is "good" and "upstanding." They may be the standout in a faith group, the kid who is dedicating herself to world causes at an early age, or the quiet child who follows the rules, gets good grades, and doesn't cause problems because they're trying to do everything "right." They struggle to have fun and enjoy age-appropriate activities. In their minds, their efforts are never good enough. These children feel increasing pressure to be more "perfect" and "morally upright." Subsequently, they lose the innocence and joys of childhood to a burden that was never theirs to begin with.

As children, they work hard at being "perfect." The Moral Hero's efforts may even be championed in the family as a way for the parent(s) to avoid their own guilt and healthy shame about what is happening. By putting the Moral Hero and Champion on a pedestal, they further entrench the child into this harmful role and pressure them to sacrifice their authentic self and feelings. A parent of a Moral Hero and Champion might say something like "Our Janie is so responsible and mature for her age. We can always trust her to make the right choices," or "Look at all he has accomplished! We must have done something right for him to turn out so well!" The child gets the message loud and clear that they are their parents' saving grace, and it is their job to continue being so. Because this sounds like praise, these children become confused and shut down feelings of anger, sadness, fear, and pain in an effort to live up to their role. The esteem they feel in being the Moral Hero and Champion comes with the heavy weight of sexual shame and pain that they are tasked with carrying for the family. The implied threat is, "If you fail to be perfect, you will no longer be loved, accepted, or important in this family."

As adults, these ACSAs continue to be drawn to roles that carry a degree of moral authority. They persist in attempting to live up to the high standards of the Moral Hero and Champion role, yet they secretly hide the shame and guilt from their own imperfect behavior. The position of pastor, priest, rabbi, judge, police officer, or lawyer allows them to crusade against the ills of the world and behave shamelessly toward others by using excessive control, judgment, and moralizing. Women are more likely to take on "softer" versions of this role, yet they may be just as sexually and morally rigid, such as the overly pious wife and mother, saintly celibate aunt, counselor, or martyr. All moral heroes present a façade of perfection, and they quarantine what they think is shameful about themselves to secret sections of their lives, where it becomes distorted. Their sexuality is a primary target.

Some characteristics of the Moral Hero and Champion include:

Being overly serious—ACSAs in the Moral Hero role assign great importance to trying to be perfect, moral, and upright in all areas of their lives: marriage, parenting, careers, and as members of the community. Succeeding at this feels like life and death to ACSAs because in childhood it truly was a matter of survival.

Rigidity regarding rules and order—They hold high standards around what they think is "right" or "wrong" and believe there are objective rules that all should live by. They are usually unforgiving toward the mistakes of others as well as themselves.

Harshly judge others and try to be "perfect"—They become harshly judgmental of others' behavior, especially regarding sexuality. Perfectionism, following the rules, and rigid morality become the structures that provide a sense of safety in an unsafe family. However, this may set ACSAs up to have secrets of their own, which they go to great lengths to hide, cover up, or deny. This "one up" position attempts to reduce the deep feelings of inadequacy that have lived inside of them since childhood.

Difficulty being playful, especially sexually—Holding onto rigid moral standards and an idea of perfection does not leave much room in ACSAs' lives for creativity, spontaneity, or play. They find being playful sexually particularly difficult, as this lies so close to their original wounding. Thus, play is most often experienced as unimportant or even dangerous because boundaries are required to protect their vulnerability, something the ACSA struggles with.

May be publicly asexual or sexually avoidant, but secretly sexual in forbidden ways—ACSAs who play the Moral Hero and Champion commonly portray themselves as being "above" sexual impulses or as having conquered them in favor of a morally righteous life. They may espouse a certain set of sexual standards but end up acting out sexually as a reaction to their own rigid rules. This creates their own conflicted cycle of guilt and shame.

RECOVERY OF THE MORAL HERO AND CHAMPION

Recovery from playing the role of the Moral Hero and Champion includes assigning rightful responsibility to each parent for their behavior, identifying and releasing the carried emotions about what happened, grieving their losses from childhood and what their own behavior cost them, and then re-parenting the various parts of self through affirmation, nurturing, and limit setting. Recovery involves creating a belief system based on embracing imperfection, learning to live within a self-defined value system, having the goal of living in forgiveness with boundaries, and ending the inaccurate belief that there is anything they can do to change or mitigate the impact of sex addiction on themselves, others, or the perception of the family. Part of the process of letting go of the shame that controls them is embracing their own human imperfection and letting go of the idea that they have to, or even *can be*, perfect. It also means acknowledging and accepting that they have been wounded, betrayed, abandoned, and enmeshed by their parents' behavior.

Additionally, it's important for the recovering Moral Hero and Champion to create their own value system, particularly with regard to their sexuality. It's helpful to keep in mind that their value system is not a reaction to their parents' behavior nor prescribed to them by society as a way to fit in or as a way to gain self-esteem. Instead, it springs forth from reestablishing connection to their authentic *self*, who intuitively knows their inherent value, knows what they think and feel, and can be responsible for their own behavior, utilizing protection and containment skills. This "owning of the self" allows ACSAs to be safe relationally and makes room for others to have their own set of morals and values. It is crucial for ACSAs to know who they are and how they want to behave, and why, outside the bounds of their role as Moral Hero or Champion within their family of origin. Finally, by letting go of this family role, they will uncover a world of self-identity, self-understanding, self-love, compassion, and joy previously unknown to them.

There are five overall goals of recovery from the Moral Champion and Hero:

Letting go of family/parental sexual shame—In recovery, ACSAs have the opportunity to learn and accept that what happened in their sexually addicted family was not their fault nor their responsibility to mitigate. Separating out the carried family shame from their own authentic emotions and being willing to be an imperfect human, like everyone else, is essential. The goal for ACSAs is to be able to say and know in their hearts, "My parents' behavior had nothing to do with me. If I thought so, I was mistaken. I let go of shame that does not belong to me."

Embrace imperfection as a normal human—ACSAs have the opportunity to learn that being human equals being imperfect. This also means they practice getting comfortable being imperfect with themselves and in front of others while simultaneously changing their internal dialogue from judgment, criticism, and disgust to warm regard, compassion, and love. In relationships with others, when ACSAs are willing to be vulnerable, they open up to the possibility of being known and loved—nurturing a growing sense of safety and ability to protect themselves with healthy boundaries. They learn to stop pretending to be superhuman.

Discovering authentic sexuality—ACSAs in recovery begin to safely explore their sexuality and sensuality outside of the negative scripts learned from their families of origin. Their goals are to be more present in their body in order to feel what they like and don't like (rather than what they think is right or wrong), to learn what safe connection with another person looks and feels like, and to dismantle shame embedded in their sexuality. They ask themselves, *What is healthy sexuality for me?*

Who do I choose to be as a man, woman, or nonbinary person? What are my beliefs about sex and sexuality? instead of *What was I taught about gender in my family of origin that I don't want to continue to believe?*

Identifying and creating authentic values—ACSAs in recovery have the opportunity to finish developing a healthy self-identity that was interrupted by the effects of their exposure to sex addiction. They discover the answers to *Who am I when I am no longer absorbed in what is right/ wrong and good/bad? What do I care about? What are the guiding principles I choose to live my life by?*

Learning how to be playful, spontaneous, and joyful—In recovery, ACSAs often, for the first time, learn how to listen to and re-parent their younger, innocent parts of self and give themselves permission to play, be creative, and have fun. As their taxed nervous systems begin to relax, they begin to open themselves to feelings of joy and peace in the body.

Chapter Six

The Comforter and Caretaker

Rosilee began therapy after being referred by HR at the primary care clinic she'd worked in as a nurse for ten years. She had been a dedicated employee who gave much of her time and attention to her patients and the practice. However, in the past year, Rosilee began to call in sick more often and seemed distracted while she was with patients. She eventually confided in a coworker that she felt overwhelmed and not herself after ending a year-long affair with one of the newer physicians in the office, Ben, who was married with two children. She felt so ashamed and embarrassed about getting involved with a married man. She thought to herself, *How did this happen? How did I get here? I'm not like one of those women my dad had affairs with. I'm a bright and educated nurse who cares about people, and helps people every day.* It brought up so many confusing thoughts and feelings inside her. Looking back, she recalls how much she enjoyed working with Ben as his nurse. He was kind and caring, so thoughtful, and gave her compliments in the way she always dreamed a man would. She felt seen and valued by him in a way she never had before. They shared a special intimacy working so closely, and before she knew it, days at the office turned into late work nights, in which he pleaded for her to stay and "help him learn the ropes." Initially she did not mind helping here and there, until the sexual tension between them could no longer be ignored. She told him nothing could come of their feelings because he was married, but he persisted until he wore her down. The relationship was like none she'd had before. She looked forward to seeing him every day, enjoyed feeling "special" and spending time together. However, she also couldn't help thinking about him going home to his wife every night after telling her he "loved" her, and that his wife "didn't understand him the way she did." She often felt sick to her stomach, had a hard time eating, and felt very lonely and confused.

She wanted to celebrate being in love, yet she could tell no one. She thought to herself, *All I ever wanted was to be in love, get married, and have a family of my own with a healthy man who was my equal partner.* Whenever she verbalized her thoughts and feelings to Ben, he would get angry, telling her he "hadn't planned on this happening, either" but begged her not to leave him. Rosilee would feel sorry for Ben, seeing his tears and pain, and believe he truly loved her. This cycle continued through the year, and nothing changed, except her. She lost twenty-five pounds, felt depressed, gave up spending time with her friends and family, and was no longer the great nurse she loved being. Meanwhile, Ben stayed married, lived in a beautiful house, was a successful physician, husband, father, and member of the community. He discounted Rosilee's thoughts and feelings, her dreams, and her goals. He only thought about himself and became hostile at work. Rosilee knew she needed to end the affair but was not confident it was really over. Rosilee was tied in knots, torn between her own longings and the sense of betrayal toward Ben's wife, who knew nothing about the affair. She was both attracted to Ben and angry at him. She felt stuck.

In therapy, whenever Ben and the situation at work was brought up, Rosilee found herself drifting back to her parents' relationship. When she was a child, her mother was always preoccupied with her dad and his chronic infidelity. Rosilee remembered feeling sorry for her mother and "felt" her broken heart. Even though she was only eight when her mother first told her about her dad's infidelity, Rosilee did everything she could to help her mom "feel better." She would often lie in bed at night, listening to her mom cry in the next room when her dad was "working late." Often, she would go to her mom to comfort her, as her mom shared about her marriage. It was one of the only times she felt close to her mother, and it felt so good when her mother praised her for being "wise beyond her years." On occasion, Rosilee would go on late-night drives with her mom to see if they would find her dad's car at work or at his affair partner's house. She felt important and trusted by her mother and excited to be out late investigating with her, but she also felt a heavy sadness at the pit of her stomach, like something wasn't right. Rosilee knew, though, that in a few days her dad would be back at home, her mom would feel better, and she could relax and go back to playing with her friends, at least for a while.

As time went on, her mother became more and more depressed. When her dad was home, her mother was focused on him, trying to make him happy, but when he was gone, she was in her room or watching TV. Rosilee learned to prepare meals for her three brothers and do the laundry. She was angry at her dad for lying and making her mother so sad, but she never told him that. Instead, she would take out her frustrations on her younger brothers, who she often had to care for while her parents were occupied elsewhere. However, Rosilee reflected in therapy, becoming a "second mother" to her brothers had helped her become responsible and mature, and it had felt good to be so needed and depended on by her family. She also admitted she would have liked to spend more time with her friends, explore her own interests, and figure out what she wanted to do with her life.

In high school, Rosilee didn't really date anyone because she was always busy helping out at home, trying to "fix" what had gone wrong in her family—be the missing piece that would make her family whole again. She believed that if she just worked hard enough, she could make things better for herself and her family. She also believed that all men were untrustworthy, and she didn't want to end up like her mother, so she just avoided them. She was sure to dress in baggy clothes, and she hated her body when she looked in the mirror. She didn't want attention from boys because it felt like they would never see her for who she was but rather as a sex object, the way her father seemed to see women.

As she became an adult, she had a few relationships, each with emotionally unavailable men who had little respect for her. She stayed in these relationships too long because she felt sorry for them and wanted to help them grow into the people she believed they could become. She held on to the fantasy that she could change them. That never happened, though, and they eventually ended the relationship with her. She also continued to feel emotionally tied to her parents' relationship, and she struggled to focus on developing her own likes and dislikes, meeting her own needs and wants, and building a fulfilling life of her own. To her therapist, she divulged, "I feel stuck, like my life is not my own! Why can't I seem to find what everyone else has?"

Roselee was set up for this "stuck" place because she was praised and rewarded with love and attention from her mother while at the same time experiencing neglect and emotional abuse. She unconsciously denied her own needs and focused on making sure her mother was "okay" because she was the safer one. She was terrified of her father. He was clearly concerned with only himself, so she stayed out of his way. She turned her sadness, fear, and anger toward her parents inward and carried a secret grief and rage inside. She acted these out in her adult life by alternating between overeating and denying herself food, and by finding relationships in which she felt intense attraction, intense fear, and inadequacy. Without realizing it, she blamed herself for the way other people treated her.

With her therapist's help, Rosilee began to see how her parents' dysfunctional patterns forced her into the role of a Comforter and Caretaker in the sexually addicted family, at the expense of her own self-development and care. Her "please and appease" behavior allowed her to survive the emotional and sexual violations in her family of origin, and then became her primary way of relating in her intimate relationships as an adult. Rosilee came to see that her relationship with Ben was just a reenactment of this pattern from childhood, where she was caught between the natural longing for a loving partnership of her own and sacrificing herself in a relationship with someone who was unavailable and self-seeking.

Rosilee worked hard in therapy on valuing herself as equal to others, learning how to identify and meet her own needs and wants, and creating and developing healthy boundaries. She learned to tolerate others' feelings of disappointment, sadness, and anger when she said "no," and not take on their painful words of control and manipulation so she could stay true to her choices. With time and practice, she felt a sense of safety, freedom, and happiness she had not experienced before. With the support of her therapist and women in her group therapy, she was able to separate herself from unhealthy involvement in her parents' relationship, as well as her relationship with Ben. She experienced feelings of fear, sadness, grief, loss, and loneliness as both her parents and Ben didn't like the new changes in her. She leaned into her support system even more by participating in activities she liked, calling them when she missed Ben, recording affirmations to re-parent herself, and focusing on moving toward her dreams for a healthy, safe, mutually nurturing relationship with an available partner.

DESCRIPTION AND CHARACTERISTICS OF THE COMFORTER AND CARETAKER

In sexually addicted families, one parent is often acting out while the other is preoccupied with their partner's acting-out behavior. As a result, neither adult is present in their primary role as a parent to guide, nurture, and protect their children. The behavior of the addicted parent leaves a large and dangerous void the whole family feels. When major caregivers abandon and neglect their primary responsibility, the system becomes unstable, and pressure builds for someone else to step in and fill this role. Inevitably, one of the children is seduced into taking care of their parent(s), their siblings, and the household responsibilities. They may become their mom's "confidant," their dad's "comforter," or a sibling's caretaker. They begin trying to take care of other people's physical, emotional, or intellectual needs in order to feel a sense of safety and security that is missing in their own parent-child relationship. The unconscious thought process is "Mom or Dad is checked out/distracted/overwhelmed/sad, etc., and someone's got to take care of things. If I help them with their problem, maybe I will get what I need."

Comforting and caretaking children are severely neglected and unconsciously become needless and wantless. They find ways to meet their needs on their own since they cannot depend on their major caregivers. The safety-seeking behavior of comforting or caretaking others goes uncorrected by parents and is instead praised. The child feels loved and valued when they are meeting their parents' needs or picking up the slack, and they are encouraged to continue in this maladaptive role. Often, the only time they receive praise, attention, or love is when they are caretaking their parents in some way.

When children witness and experience boundary violations, abandonment, betrayal, and neglect through a parent's infidelity, they replicate the same learned behavior. In their innocence, they have no choice but to violate their own boundaries and abandon and betray themselves in order to stabilize their unstable parent(s). The child feels chronically in need of more love and attention from others and feels helpless in securing their own interests. They caretake others as a way to feel needed, wanted, and loved. Thus, the role of Comforter and Caretaker gives the child a false sense of power, which leads to living in extremes and believing they can meet their own needs. As adults, they take on too much responsibility, isolate themselves emotionally, and do not ask for help from others. They may appear to "have it all together" but are actually suffering silently and alone.

This role reversal is incredibly damaging to a child, despite immediate appearances, and causes long-term confusion and pain in the areas of self-esteem, boundary systems, connection to their body, knowledge of their own thoughts and feelings, responsibility for their own behavior, identification of needs versus wants, and a life of living in extremes. It robs children of their innocence, security, and sense of being safe and cared for.

A comforting and caretaking child gets caught in a trap of enmeshment they cannot see, let alone escape. The unspoken job of this child is to take care of or stabilize their needy parent. Sadly, they carry this role into their adult relationships and are often drawn to careers based on this pattern. They continue to caretake their parents, siblings, friends, coworkers, and others, often at the expense of their own self-care. The core beliefs persist, *If I do this for you, you will finally see me, hear me, value me, and love me*; or *I know what's best for you. I will tell you who you need to be for my comfort, and you'll thank me and love me as a result.* This is flawed thinking and creates a multitude of issues in adult relationships.

The Comforter and Caretaker role has the following characteristics in common:

Believe it's their job to be responsible for, fix, and/or stabilize other people emotionally—ACSAs in this role have an "other" orientation that leads to over-responsibility, boundary violations, and enmeshment in other people's issues at the expense of their own self-care. They hold the inaccurate belief that they will get their own needs and wants met if they can meet the needs and wants of other people. They are trying to establish safety and security, where it is otherwise lacking, by doing the job of the absent or neglectful parent(s) and thus feeling "useful." Their stepping into the caregiver's job as parent can go unnoticed, be praised and valued, or end in being shamed and scapegoated by the caregivers if they confront the truth of the addiction. The Comforter and Caretaker adult child often stays in the background but finds herself "on call" and ready to step in to stabilize whatever deficit or emergency the family system needs.

Carry pain, fear, anger, shame, and loneliness—Children of sex addicts overidentify with the betrayed parent and try to soothe the pain, fear, anger, shame, and loneliness caused by the sex addict's betrayal, taking it on as their own. But, because these emotions are too overwhelming to manage in their young bodies, they come to believe they are the problem. They have learned an unconscious belief that *If I sit down, be quiet, and be who my mom and dad need me to be, everything will be all right,* or *I will be loved,* or *I will be safe.* Thus, they continue displacing this core belief onto others in adulthood by thinking *You need to sit down, be quiet, and be who I need you to be, so I don't have to look at my own shame-based belief system.* As a defense against the carried shame, ACSAs displace their feelings onto others and may hold others in contempt or judgment.

Conditional sense of self—ACSAs' self-esteem is based on how useful they are to their family members and others in their lives. Their sense of self comes from giving to others, not from a sense of inherent worth. They constantly "hustle" to earn their worth and value, at a cost to their own dreams and interests.

Drawn romantically to partner with a "sex addict"—Having overidentified with the betrayed partner, ACSAs often carry the unconscious need to resolve and repair what was disrupted in their family of origin. They may be unknowingly attracted to partners who will help them create similar emotional circumstances until the core wounds from childhood are healed. Alternatively, some comforter/caretakers become sexually addicted themselves.

Difficulty protecting themselves from unsafe people or circumstances—
Due to lack of protection in their families of origin, ACSAs do not learn healthy and safe boundaries. They tend to display an innocence or naivety that leaves them unable to detect unsafe people or circumstances. With the difficulty in protecting themselves emotionally, they can be impetuous, involving themselves before they determine whether the person is safe.

RECOVERY OF THE COMFORTER AND CARETAKER

In order for ACSAs to move out of the role of Comforter and Caretaker, they must first develop the ability to see their role in their family of origin, as well as its harmful effects on their lives and development. They must identify and come to terms with the painful truth that their "helpfulness" to others is a self-defeating behavior. Because ACSAs give of themselves repeatedly and do not receive the same in return, they do not find the unconditional love and acceptance they are longing for. Healing also requires a fundamental restructuring or often a complete creation of self, with guidance from their wiser, spiritual self and their own value system. ACSAs must affirm new beliefs: "I was created precious, worthwhile, and valuable simply because I was born. I am equal to every person I encounter, and they are equal to me. I'm not better than, and I'm not less than." These new foundational beliefs allow ACSAs to value themselves before others, and subsequently, they learn to connect to their bodies, identify and express feelings, set boundaries, honor others' boundaries, cultivate a support system, ask for help, verbalize needs and wants without feeling shame or guilt, and replace old patterns with new, healthier ways of thinking, relating, and living. In order to heal, these ACSAs have to learn how to come to their own assistance, listen to their bodies, emotionally regulate and soothe in healthy ways, and care for their own needs as a first priority.

There are four overall goals of recovery from the Comforter and Caretaker role:

Rediscover inherent self-worth/self-esteem—ACSAs must make the difficult shift from thinking they are only valuable when giving to others to internally knowing they are enough no matter what. They must practice esteeming themselves from within, even—and especially—when they experience inevitable pushback from those they used to caretake. Affirmations, relational support, and work with a wiser, spiritual self are very helpful as this new value system is being developed.

Develop self-protection and containment—Moving away from the Comforter and Caretaker role involves creating healthy boundary systems. ACSAs must say "no" when they mean "no" and learn to live with others being upset, angry, or disappointed. They must accept the possibility of losing the relationship. Healing also means maintaining a sense of self, remembering, *It is not my job to take care of needy people*, and learning how to discern when they can "help" or assist others when it doesn't take away from themselves. ACSAs must ask for their needs to be met and learn to tolerate "no" if someone cannot meet their needs.

Detect blind spots—ACSAs have to identify the template of their parents' betrayal cycle, which was the only "love" they knew growing up and, therefore, becomes one of their blind spots in relationships. For example,

if an ACSA watched her mother get frantic with anxiety and tears when her husband stayed out all night, then witnessed him return the next day in tears, remorseful, begging for his wife's forgiveness, the ACSA will feel the broken heart of one or both parents. Because she witnessed their cycle of betrayal, filled with intense emotions of anxiety, pain, and anger, she felt resentful toward one parent and "felt sorry" for the other.

ACSAs must untangle the rationalizations and stories told to them by each parent because this is where they are most vulnerable and seducible. Others can get in and manipulate them, take advantage of their kindness, and use them without their knowledge. The goal is to see reality, get the story straight, and ask the following questions: *What's my truth about what I saw and heard from each parent? What did I learn and from whom? What was the message their behavior taught me? What was congruent, not congruent? How was I set up to act against my own self-interest? What does a relationship based on trust look like? Do I trust myself? Am I trustworthy and safe to be in a relationship with myself and others?* Only then will ACSAs be able to create a foundation of safety and trust and shift the ongoing dynamics in their adult lives.

Create a healthy support system—It is paramount for ACSAs to create a support system in which they learn they are not alone, that others have experienced the same trauma and also behaved poorly. Sharing their stories, which include their darkest secrets, to other recovering ACSAs allows them to experience the duality of being lovable and imperfect. This becomes the new foundation for their lives.

Putting self first—ACSAs must learn to put themselves at the top of their relationship list. When ACSAs have a healthy relationship with self, they become safe to themselves and can be relational with others in mature ways. Decisions are made from a place of self-love and self-care, not from a calculation of others' responses. A helpful question for Comforters and Caretakers is "Will this behavior be in my long-term best interest and support me for the next fifty years?" In other words, does this behavior or choice add to my life or take away from my life and the lives of those who love me or those that I love? Our bodies give us the answer via sensations. We learn how to listen to them.

Work through resentments—ACSAs must look at how they carried the pain, shame, anger, fear, or loneliness for their parent(s), and how they may have displaced it on themselves (depression, self-harm, body image issues, etc.) or others (fighting with siblings, rebelling against authority, raging at strangers, etc.). They also need to get in touch with their own anger toward both parents for being drawn into a painful web of abandonment, enmeshment, and neglect.

Chapter Seven

The Surrogate Spouse

John came into therapy frustrated with his wife, Susan, because she didn't seem to understand why he had to visit with his mother over the weekend. Even though he and his wife had plans for hiking and picnicking to help refresh their waning romance, John asked her to reschedule for the following weekend because his mother needed him. His mother complained that she was feeling lonely, and her arthritis was acting up. She asked John to come over on the weekend to help with some chores around the house. Although it was over a two-hour drive one-way, he agreed to do it. John knew his wife would be upset because he had canceled plans with her for his mother many other times over the course of their marriage. He was torn, but he felt too guilty not to tend to his mother when she needed him. After all, he lamented during the therapy session, he was all his mother had after his father left for another woman when John was ten years old.

Over the course of his childhood, his mother would often confide in him that she knew his dad was "with another woman." In his early years, he wasn't sure what this meant, but he sensed how lonely and sad his mother was and felt sorry for and protective of her. John reported that she would often comment to him during his father's absence, "I don't know what I would do if it wasn't for you." Though he felt burdened with his mother's woes, he had a special pride in his role as his mother's savior. After his father left, John was brokenhearted, but he thought it was best for his mother. His dad had cheated many times, and John was tired of his parents fighting. His mother leaned on him even more and often expressed her feelings of loneliness and sadness. She began to take him everywhere: shopping, to movies, out to dinner, and seemingly anywhere she needed a companion. John reported feeling bothered and trapped by this at times, even "icky"; however, he felt powerful and even more special now that he seemed to be becoming his mother's constant, loyal companion.

John did not date much during his teen years, always feeling shy and reticent to approach girls. He even felt guilty at times for wanting to date, though he didn't understand why. After high school, John attended a local community college, a choice his mother insisted on since he would be close by. Even though he wanted to go to the university across state and live on campus, he relented to his mother, knowing she would feel better with him near. He met Susan in one of his classes, and she was the one who initiated their first date. He kept the relationship largely a secret from his mother for fear that she would get jealous and protest. When he finally had the courage to introduce Susan to his mother, true to his fears, his mother expressed her displeasure to him. When Susan wasn't around, his mother began to pout and cast constant doubt to him about his choice of partner.

John felt torn and pleaded with Susan to understand his mother's feelings and do her best to warm up to her. At first, Susan thought John's concern for his mother's feelings was a good sign, and she went out of her way to befriend his mother. Eventually, John's mother seemed to accept Susan on the surface. Soon after, Susan suggested they get married, and John proposed. After John's marriage, it did not take long for his mother to start complaining to him. She felt Susan interfered with her time with John. Feeling tremendous guilt and pressure not to disappoint his mother, John tried to placate both women by sharing time between them. Susan expressed concerns that their marriage was being neglected and that she should be his priority. This began many years of arguing over his involvement with his mother, leaving Susan to accept less and less of John's commitment to the marriage. John, in his frustration and feelings of guilt provoked by both his mother and now his wife, would compulsively turn to pornographic images and videos and masturbate. He claimed it helped him feel "free" and that the women he viewed "made no demands on him." He had vowed he would "never be like his father" and felt tremendous shame when he realized he had become a version of him. Over time, he withdrew sexually from Susan, which only exacerbated her feelings of being neglected and unloved. Because they argued often, John found himself willing to attend therapy, though he largely focused on his wife's lack of understanding about his mother.

When the therapist suggested the marriage needed greater loyalty to Susan than to his mother in order for the marriage to work, John defended his involvement with his mother. Initially, he persisted in his belief that he and Susan would argue less if she could just be more understanding of his mother's feelings. Over time in the therapy process, John came to see that his mother's involvement in his life and marriage was indeed an interference. He realized it was not his job to cushion his mother's loneliness. Finally, John understood it was his mother's job to support his independence and his marriage and not to burden him with her woes. He began to set boundaries with his mother and was less and less at her beck and call. The pornography had less of a grip, and he felt more available to Susan.

John was able to separate and emancipate as his own man and still care for his mother. He needed to "divorce" the unspoken contractual agreement to be his mother's loyal companion and make himself and his wife his first priorities. And, he had to see his father on his own terms rather than as his mother wanted him to. By doing this, he created his own version of his father to identify with as well as free himself to disidentify with parts that "he" disliked.

DESCRIPTION AND CHARACTERISTICS OF THE SURROGATE SPOUSE

The adult coupleship in sexually addicted families is unfulfilling to one or both of the partners, leaving them feeling lonely and empty. The spouse of the sex addict feels dismissed, unwanted, and disempowered. Seeking comfort, security, and a sense of control, they turn to one of the children to fill the role of the surrogate husband or wife. They exert control over the life of the child as a way to compensate for feeling helpless and victimized by the sex addict. They also use the child's love and devotion that are natural in early childhood years to mold the child into a loyal companion to replace the loss of the adult partner caused by the sex addiction. The parent may also use the child to "show up" the neglectful, sexually addicted partner. This creates unneeded competition and resentment that causes distance between the child and the other parent. The sexually addicted parent might also use the child to run interference for him, so he can "act out" his sex addiction; *for example*, "you take care of your mother for me." In either case, the child loses out on one parent and is controlled and dominated by the other.

This domination is costly to the child. They are left feeling loyal out of obligatory guilt and learn to tune in to the feelings and needs of the lonely parent at a cost to their own strivings for independence, self-actualization, and romantic and sexual interests. They feel trapped and engulfed. They learn to compromise, so as to remain available and loyal to the parent, rationalizing and defending the parent's intrusiveness and control. However, the compromises are designed to placate the needy parent in hopes of garnering currency that will finally set them free. It never works, and their lives lack passion and purpose.

The opening story of the Surrogate Spouse is a heterosexual man loyal to his mother, though there are variations on this theme that have some differences. However, the core issue of guilty loyalty at a cost to their own lives is central to all the variations. A woman can find herself in the role of her mother's "best friend" and constant companion to replace an absent husband due to sex addiction. She feels special but trapped and smothered. Compulsive eating may become her way of exercising a degree of control and false sense of freedom; *for example*, "You can't control my eating; I'll eat what I want!" She will absorb her mother's anger at her father and make it hers. She then projects it out onto other men and finds it difficult to have a successful romance, all the while staying loyal to her mom. Culturally, women are more often expected to take care of the parents, which adds to the loyalty burden and the difficulty charting their own lives in the way they wish.

Women can also find themselves playing the role of their sexually addicted father's special "girlfriend," leading to their own sexual issues and romantic difficulties. We address this more in the chapter on the Seducer. Or, if the mother is sexually addicted, the daughter may fill the loneliness of her father by becoming his Comforter and Caretaker. In some instances, women can be both their mother's companion and father's special "girl-friend." In this case, the identity of the young girl is lost under the weight of these Surrogate Spouse role assignments.

Gay men can find themselves in the role of their mother's companion as well. They are similar to heterosexual men in many ways, particularly in the feelings of being trapped. However, they often defend the relationship with their mothers, as she may have been the only parent on their side once they "came out" with being gay. Lesbian women who were a companion or Surrogate Spouse to their father have also reported he was the only one there for them once their orientation was known. Other aspects can differ from heterosexual men and women and should be considered when sorting the Surrogate Spouse role. LGBTQ+ and nonbinary people will need to sort this out as it pertains to their specific circumstances.

All the variations on the theme of playing the role of Surrogate Spouse to a parent have characteristics in common, which include the following:

Feeling loyal to parents over a romantic partner—ACSAs who have played the Surrogate Spouse role will feel more loyal to their parents

than to their romantic partners, creating ongoing conflict and romantic dissatisfaction.

Excessive feelings of guilty obligation and people-pleasing—Because ACSAs feel responsible and obligated to the parent, they often project obligatory guilt onto many circumstances in their lives and try to please by meeting others' needs. They say "yes" to others' requests, even when the decision is not in their own interests.

Indecisiveness and a lost sense of self—ACSAs' needs and desires may have merged with their parents' needs, leaving them uncertain as to how they feel about important decisions that require an "inner knowing." Their sense of identity has been controlled and shaped by their parents' needs, leaving them to take cues from others as to how they should define themselves. They are enmeshed in their parents' lives and identity at a cost to their own.

Difficulty with commitments—They commit quickly before "vetting" a person or situation and then struggle to back out, often remaining loyal longer than is good for them. Or they hold back commitments, always "leaving the door open for escape," even in the most benign of situations.

Romantic and sexual struggles—Feeling "married" to their parent and loyal to the role of the stable "Surrogate Spouse who will never leave," ACSAs struggle to navigate a fully satisfying sexual and romantic life.

Addictions—Addictions, particularly to food and sex, can be seen as a false promise of freedom. While ACSAs feel controlled and trapped by the parent, they may rebel with the pursuit of addictive behaviors as a way to counter the entrapment.

RECOVERY OF THE SURROGATE SPOUSE

Recovery from playing the role of the Surrogate Spouse to a parent must include ACSAs' ending of the implicit and explicit contractual arrangements to "give up their lives for their parents." ACSAs often confuse this assignment with "amputating" the parent and then feel guilty. Subsequently, they refuse to change the contract, leaving them feeling stuck and unable to move forward. The goal is for them to break free and still love their parents but put themselves and their spouses or partners first on the list of priorities.

There are four overall goals of recovery from the Surrogate Spouse role:

Separation—This includes boundaries regarding time, touch, visits, and topics of conversations with the parent or "proxies" of the parent, such as a brother or sister who is doing the parent's bidding.

Differentiation—The feelings, needs, worries, and anxieties of the ACSAs' parents do not belong to the ACSAs. ACSAs are "different" from their parents. Learning to stay detached and caring with their parents without taking on their problems is an important internal boundary to help differentiate themselves and leave them free to chart their own life course.

Emancipation—ACSAs need a clear commitment of loyalty to themselves, their romantic partners, their families of procreation, and their careers or working paths that is greater than the loyalty to their parents or families of origin. There is no way around this shift in loyalties if they want a fulfilled life. Many ACSAs try to "even out" the loyalties, which is also doomed for conflict and greater unhappiness. Parents who truly have their adult child's best interests in mind lovingly bless this change and learn to negotiate with them this new arrangement of loyalties.

Individuation—Finally, ACSAs need to learn to individuate by being their own persons in their friendships and romantic relationships. ACSAs who have played the roles of Surrogate Spouses often have re-created the dynamic of the enmeshed entanglement with their spouses or partners by displacing feelings about their moms or dads onto their beloved ones. Thus, the individuation of self as it relates to their partners will be critical to recovery so that ACSAs are not reacting to their partners as if the ACSAs are being controlled or trapped.

Chapter Eight

The Seducer and Addict

At the age of twenty-six, Hannah estimated she had been with "too many sexual partners" to count. She had a long-term boyfriend, Austin, whom she was unable to be faithful to in their on-and-off again romance. She dreamed of marriage and kids one day, but neither she nor Austin trusted her to be true to wedding vows. When she suggested that the answer was an "open marriage," Austin broke it off and, for the first time in their history, would not return her desperate calls or texts. Certain he was moving on, Hannah had what she described as a "breakdown," crying often and feeling increasingly depressed. Finally, unable to ward off the pain of her loss, she entered therapy, looking for help.

In her early sessions, Hannah oscillated between regret and defensiveness, as she talked of what she described as Austin's rejection of her. She didn't understand why he wouldn't consider an open marriage, though she had read of others who had done it and felt it would be the best solution for them to stay together. Unable to see her own lack of empathy, she persisted in defending her position—until she was asked to be specific as to the type of encounters in which she was primarily attracted. With an obvious display of shame, Hannah described that she was almost always drawn to seducing married (or "taken") men and experienced a degree of satisfaction in causing pain to the wife and destruction to the marriage that she had violated. Once the man wanted her over the wife and became willing to leave the marriage, she would reject him and escape back to the comfort of her relationship with Austin, who was largely unaware of the specifics of her pattern. It was in this admission that she began to take stock of the pain and problems she caused herself and others and soon admitted she "could not control herself."

When asked how this pattern of seducing married men began, Hannah revealed long-held feelings of pain, anger, confusion, and shame over her father's many affairs and the betrayal to her mother, which were both center stage in the family's dysfunction during her childhood. Her father always seemed to be charming to the women he met, even when Hannah's mother was present. Hannah's mother would get jealous and angry, then start a fight with Hannah's father. Hannah hated the fighting and would often blame her mother for the problems, even though she knew what her father was doing was wrong.

In time, Hannah wanted her father to pay special attention to her, rather than the other women, and would go out of her way as a teen to ask her dad if she "looked pretty" when she would wear makeup and get dressed up. While her father would pay attention to her briefly, he seldom stayed around the house and would leave to be with "his women."

Feeling rejected, Hannah would vow to try even harder next time to get her father to notice her. As her mother saw more of this attention seeking, she became increasingly jealous of Hannah, often expressing scorn and anger toward her, which resulted in Hannah siding with her father despite his adulterous behavior.

In high school, Hannah started feeling compelled to "steal" other girls' boyfriends. While this created problems for her socially, Hannah enjoyed her power to seduce boys and cause hurt to other girls. Privately, she despised herself when her current "cycle of seduction ended," yet she felt helpless to stop. Upon entering college, she vowed she would stop her seduction. For a while, though still fighting urges to seduce, she was able to refrain from her pattern of seduction.

She met Austin in one of her classes, dated him for a short time, and quickly fell in love. Hannah felt she could finally put her seductive past behind her, now that she had found her "true love." They enjoyed months of romance and "good sex." However, Hannah soon found herself thinking of seducing other women's men to "get even" if she felt misunderstood by Austin, even during minor arguments. Over time, her seductive pattern began again, only this time, she was more discreet by meeting men through apps and making sure they were not part of her social circle. She began living two lives, with Austin periodically becoming aware of her betrayals. Each time, Hannah was able to "talk her way out of it" by lying, blaming, and gaslighting Austin. But the loss of Austin was a grief that she could not "talk her way out of," even to herself.

Over time in her therapy, Hannah began to see the connection between her own compulsive, seductive behavior and her father's sex addiction. While she was angry with him for his adulterous behavior, she was drawn to the power he seemed to wield by this behavior and his dismissiveness toward her mother, whom she felt contempt for and distanced from. At one "aha" moment in therapy, she sadly recalled saying to herself as a young teen, "I'd much rather be like my dad than a victim like my mother." Further driven by her need to get her father's attention over the "other women," her seductive pursuit of "taken men" was put in place. By hurting other women along the way, she could also act out and displace her anger toward her mother onto these women, further entrenching her seductive pattern. Hannah had become like her father—addicted to sex and using her seductive powers to give herself a sense of control, which helped her counter the helplessness left from her childhood and defend against the internal threat of becoming a victim like her mother.

Hannah's therapy focused on helping her see that her seductive self was the part of her "left behind in the childhood drama" she was traumatized by, though still very present and largely in charge of her romantic and sexual decisions. She focused on learning about this part of herself and expressing her pent-up feelings of sadness and anger. She was able, for the first time, to tell her father how angry she was with him for betraying her and her mother. This enabled Hannah to lose some of the power behind her own desire to seduce. She also reconciled her feelings toward her mother and made amends to her for unfairly blaming her for the family dysfunction. By making peace with and having empathy for her mother, Hannah was able to see her as more than a victim and to allow herself the long overdue need to identify with her mother's strengths and passions. In turn, her empathy for her mother grew and, thus, diminished her need to both see other women as competition and to secure the attention of unavailable men in order to affirm her worth.

Two other aspects of Hannah's healing became critical. One was her recognition that she had an addiction to sex like her father. But unlike him, she began the process of recovery by attending support groups, programs, and communities aimed at helping her recover from engaging in her destructive, addictive patterns (see Resource section for group contacts). Part of this recovery journey was to grieve the loss of Austin and make amends to him. While Hannah had hoped he might give her another chance, he didn't. She then took the second critical piece of her recovery, which was to declare and commit herself to a new set of values and behaviors that would guide her romantic and sexual decisions going forward. In doing so, Hannah restored her hope that one day she could be married and have the family she'd always dreamed of.

DESCRIPTION AND CHARACTERISTICS OF THE SEDUCER AND ADDICT

Fundamental to understanding the link between ACSAs' sexuality and their family systems is the concept that "developmental input often matches biographic output." In other words, sexual expression is often a function of the type of early developmental experiences that occurred in childhood and are assimilated into the developing sexuality of the children. When growing up, if children witness love, appropriate touch, healthy messages around sexuality, and safe displays of romantic expression, their sexuality unfolds naturally and is used in the service of love, attachment, and safe play. In contrast, ACSAs' experiences of sexuality growing up reflect a lack of safety and appropriate touch, and instead, consist of addictive sex and excessive conflict regarding sexual matters. Along with fear-based, rigid-moral, and/or excessively permissive messaging about sexual matters, ACSAs' sexuality is often shame based and conflicted. ACSAs' sexuality is more an internalized expression of the conflicted sexual stories of their parents than a true unfolding of the natural expression of their own desires. Sex becomes a tool to act out the forbidden, discharge anger and grievances, and cover pain and loss.

The Seducer and Addict in the sexually addicted family system has identified with the sex addict, often the dominant parent with more observable power in the family system. The sexually addicted parent becomes more attractive to align with because the other parent is often seen as weak and without power. This is the devastating effect of betrayal trauma. Like in Hannah's story, the Seducer and Addict is well guarded against becoming what they perceive as helpless, weak, and too vulnerable and will go to great lengths to defend and hold on to the role. The threat of the fragile sense of self collapsing under the weight of what appears to be a victim role or position of powerlessness is so great that the Seducer and Addict's "agenda" takes over, despite shame and negative consequences. Even while declaring, "I will never be like him (or her)," the ACSA becomes a version of the sexually addicted parent.

To clarify, ACSAs can be addicted to sex without being the Seducer. For example, addiction to pornography or online sexual activity can be a way to play out the role of the Addict. Here, the sexual activity is done in greater degrees of privacy where the threat of rejection is minimized while still allowing the ACSA to feel sexually powerful and in control. What this version has in common with the overt Seducer is the identification with the sexually addicted parent as a position of power that mitigates against the helplessness carried from their family dysfunction. Addictive sex becomes a tool to ward off loss, pain, and helplessness and to discharge anger and shame.

In other words, an ACSA can also be sexually addicted without being in the role of the Seducer. In this case, the ACSA has taken on the role of the sex addict, identifying with the power position of the sexually addicted parent, but adding to the burden of shame as a result of their own sexual behavior. This may distract the ACSA from facing the sexual shame of the family by becoming the "carrier of the shame," further protecting the family from seeing the role of the parent's sex addiction. This ACSA may be scapegoated as the "bad one," whom the family focuses on as the one who brings shame onto the family, thereby taking the focus off the role of the parent. This ACSA must get into their own recovery from addiction in order to begin to see clearly the impact of the family.

The variations of identifying with the sexually addicted parent have the following characteristics in common:

Use sex to express pain and anger and defend against a fragile sense of self—Having witnessed sex used as a commodity by the sexually addicted parent, ACSAs use sex as a tool to defend the sense of self against interpersonal threat or to discharge anger resulting from perceived or actual slights or grievances, often regarding themes of unfairness.

"I will never be like him (or her)"—This is a frequent declaration by ACSAs as an attempt not to become like the sexually addicted parent themselves. However, this declaration is no match for the impact that the sex addiction had on the child's development. They shut down sexually or are drawn to the taboo situations that the sexually addicted parent modeled for them. They may also oscillate between these two extremes.

Hold in contempt, and keep distance from, the spouse of the sex addict—Too often, the spouse of the sex addict is the focal point of anger and conflict. The trauma associated with being married to or involved with a sex

addict causes acute distress and high reactivity in the spouse, whereby they often are seen as the one creating the conflict in the family. ACSAs often hold the spouse of the sex addict unfairly responsible by seeing this parent as an unnecessary victim as well as the one responsible for starting family fights. This view contributes to the overidentification with the sex addict.

Become sexually addicted and reenact their parent's sexually addictive behavior—ACSAs may become addicted themselves to sex. Despite the negative consequences and mounting losses, ACSAs struggle to admit their addiction because they never want to become like their sexually addicted parent. Like most sex addicts, ACSAs' sexual expression is not a loving and playful expression of self to be shared with a beloved. Instead, it is an internalized battleground of conflicts that were never supposed to be their burden in the first place. Their sexual expression and arousal become increasingly dependent on control, power, and ritualistic behavior and can repeat their parent's sexual behavior.

Difficulty with gender role identity (this is different than sorting biologically assigned gender and should not be viewed in that context)— Gender roles in sexually addicted families are often rigid and overly sexualized. ACSAs find themselves being overly competitive with the same gender, pursuing sexual conquests to validate gender roles, dismissing more vulnerable and necessary aspects of their gender, compensating for feelings of gender inadequacies through sexually addictive behavior, and/or attempting to fit into rigid gender roles. ACSAs identifying as nonbinary people or LGBTQ+ will need to sort this aspect as it relates to their specific circumstances to determine in what way their parent's sex addiction impacted their own unique identity.

RECOVERY OF THE SEDUCER AND ADDICT

Recovery from the Seducer and Addict role, or the more generalized role of sex addict, involves facing the reality that the role is a carryover from childhood and contains the sexually addicted family story displayed and acted out in the sexual behavior of the ACSAs. It means facing this reality and separating from the shameful burdens and assigned values and behaviors that were not the ACSAs' choosing, and then, committing to a new sexual and romantic path of their choice.

The overall goals of recovery from the Seducer and Addict role include:

Disinheriting yourself from your parent's sex addiction path and the legacy of unresolved sexual shame from the family—Disinheriting is

a strong word, but it reflects the reality that ACSAs must make an absolute commitment to change the trajectory of their sexual journey, even if that means being misunderstood or disenfranchised by members of their sexually addicted families. New boundaries must be set. It might include something as simple as not laughing at the sexual jokes bantered around at family get-togethers to more confrontational ones, like not participating in visits nor allowing unsupervised time with the grandchildren unless there are significant changes in the behavior of the sexually addicted parent. These expected changes may also include other family members who are aligned with the dysfunction of the system. The commitment must be to the separation from the sexually addicted system dynamics and not seeking approval from the parents, even if that means loss. Compromising this position will invite the sexually addicted system dynamics to hold sway in matters of the heart. Values that reflect a new definition of the role of sexuality in the ACSA's life will need to be clarified.

Facing addiction—Loss of control, negative consequences, and continuation of the behavior despite the consequences are a simple way to determine if sex addiction is present. If so, addiction treatment approaches along with self-help groups offer the best chance for recovery (see Resource section for group contacts). Promises and self-will, no matter how sincere, usually fail in trying to stop an addiction. Addiction treatment recovery establishes a path of letting go of what is not working and invites a commitment to a path of hope and possibility. In the case of ACSAs, that means coming to believe in the hope that a healthy intimacy and a satisfying sexuality, free of the shame of the past, are possible.

Creating a new sexual path—ACSAs have grown up within an overly sexualized atmosphere. As a result, the Seducer and Addict have overvalued sex at the cost of love. For these ACSAs, a new sexuality rests in the willingness to let love shape sex and for sex to invite love.

Chapter Nine

The Truth Teller

We have observed a dynamic around "telling the truth" that warrants further consideration. This is not an adaptation to the sexually addicted family like the previous four roles. Instead, the truth telling can occur in childhood or later in the ACSA recovery process. The Truth Teller in the family is the child who is striving to retain their truth against the denial of parental sex addiction. Later, in ACSA recovery, it is a transitional phase from being trapped in one's assigned family role to authenticity.

In sexually addicted families, children's natural openness is often shut down out of fear that parents will abandon or shame them for "telling the truth." In each of the previously described roles, there is a shutting down of the child's authentic thoughts, feelings, and behavior. Children begin hiding and losing connection with parts of themselves. Losing the ability to tell the truth about what is happening in the family is a symptom of this loss.

Children who resist the pressure to give in to their family role assignments become scapegoated. For example, parents may say, "Do as I say, not as I do." When the children point out this incongruence, the parents will experience a perceived blow to their self-esteem and react in extremes. In one extreme they go into a "one up" position and rage, blame, criticize, attack, humiliate, or get even—all forms of shaming. In the other extreme, the parents take themselves into the "one down" position and behave from a victim-like stance—crying, begging for forgiveness, and vowing to stop—creating a bind internally so the children end up feeling sorry for them.

Parents who scapegoat the children as the "problem" are hiding from responsibility for their own shameful behavior. For example, a future Comforter and Caretaker may try to get help outside the family and be scapegoated for revealing family secrets. Children who try to retain their truthful authenticity are likely to be blamed, shamed, attacked, and even rejected by the family until they comply. Parents avoid taking responsibility because they don't know how to manage their own feelings and so displace their pain, shame, fear, and loneliness onto the child instead. The truth is silenced by scapegoating the children.

When recovering ACSAs begin to "de-role," similar situations occur. Family members often protest the truth telling by accusing the ACSAs of being disloyal, stirring up trouble, being dishonest, or not doing their job of "fixing" the addict's broken heart. There are times when distance from family members is necessary for self-protection. A parent in recovery might be able to welcome their adult child's point of view, take responsibility for their mistakes, and process their feelings. Unfortunately, many ACSAs will not find the family validation they hope for as they heal.

The following are recovery recommendations for ACSAs as they navigate the Truth Telling phase of recovery:

Don't take on the injustices of the world—Recovering ACSAs can become overly vigilant to injustices, especially when it comes to sexual morality. It is helpful for ACSA's to first focus on affirming the self and creating boundaries while softening to the world around them and learning to tolerate mistakes and imperfection in themselves and others.

Build safe, supportive, reciprocal relationships—ACSAs need solid support systems and robust social lives where they can learn how to be themselves and practice shielded vulnerability. It is important to build a "family of choice" that includes people who are on a healing journey of their own and demonstrate safety, trustworthiness, healthy boundaries, the ability to repair relational ruptures maturely and live within their emotional and sexual value systems.

Avoid getting romantically involved with people who reenact the family dynamics—ACSAs are able to choose healthier partners when they recognize their childhood role assignments. They can learn to notice red flags if behavior choices replicate patterns from childhood and practice new skills relationally until the new behavior becomes a well-worn path. *Set emotional limits and/or get physical distance from family members, colleagues, and friends*—ACSAs must be able to recognize when scapegoating, gaslighting, and abuse are happening and take action to protect themselves.

Seek support from a trained therapist and other ACSAs—Truth telling is emotionally taxing and can feel overwhelming at times. The process can bring up traumatic wounds and difficult realizations. It is crucial for ACSAs to have knowledgeable guides and strong support.

Grieve losses and rightfully assign responsibility—It is important to acknowledge losses caused by parental sex addiction, and to allow all feelings the time and space needed, ACSAs need to tell the truth about how they were impacted and "give back" any anger, fear, shame, and pain that did not belong to them. This can be done with or without their parents' involvement.

ACSAs must stand in their truth, even if their parents are unable to hear it or are unwilling to validate their experiences and make amends. Their families' inability to act lovingly is not the ACSAs' fault or responsibility. They cannot allow this to silence them. Telling the truth in a sexually addicted family is an act of bravery. When ACSAs speak their truth, honor their experiences, develop a healthy relationship with themselves and live their own lives, it creates a sense of empowerment and freedom to live in the present.

On this journey, it is essential to value and affirm the different ages of the child parts within, who want to speak the truth, be loved, and be free to be themselves. As a recovery exercise, ACSAs can affirm: "Even though my family doesn't support me, I am courageous, honest, and lovable. I am learning to act in integrity with my values. I am becoming loyal to my innermost truth, and I am following the way when all others abandon it. I am walking the path of my own heart."

Chapter Ten

Healing and Recovery

The primary healing and recovery objective for ACSAs is to unburden the legacy of sexual shame created by the sex addicts' behaviors, secrets, and shamefulness that infiltrated the family systems. ACSAs' sexuality has been organized around their reaction to the sex addicts' behaviors and lack of shame as well as the betrayed partners, anxiety, sadness, and grief. As we have seen in the ACSA role descriptions, they may be overcontrolled sexually as a means to counter the shame and pain of either parent, or they may become permissive and irresponsible in their behavior as a way to identify with the power that the sex addict held and to counter their own sense of helplessness.

While each role has its own recovery, as detailed in previous chapters, the following can serve as general recovery guidelines:

- **Break through denial**—Children growing up in homes that are abusive, addictive, or dysfunctional normalize the behaviors of their parents, even when those behaviors cause shame or pain. Over time, these behaviors feel "familiar" to the child, and they begin to deny the inappropriateness of their parents' behaviors as well as their own feelings and reality. They learn to deny that which is unacceptable or painful. They will defend this unacceptable behavior as "normal" or "not that bad" to themselves and to others who attempt to help or confront the addictive system.

    Denial, a cushion against the intolerable weight of sexual shame caused by the addict, now becomes its own problem. ACSAs who have learned to use denial to cope, struggle to negotiate effectively in relationships, have poor social skills, have limited compassion and empathy, find it difficult to practice self-care, don't attune to cues from others, nor effectively protect themselves in the face of dangerous or problematic relationships. ACSAs must break through denial by gently and persistently guiding the part of them that has not wanted to feel and see the truth—to allow the reality of the sex addiction and its impact to become more conscious—or allow even small aspects of the truth to emerge if the entire story feels too overwhelming.

    It is important for ACSAs to assign the appropriate

responsibility for the shame where it belongs: on the sex addict's behavior. They must seek support from those who are not invested in denying their family's sex addiction. Siblings, while having lived in the same family, are not always good supporters as they have their own denial of the truth. Find a therapist, support group, and/ or friend who will validate your feelings and reality.

- **Personalize the recovery suggestions**—We have outlined the most salient characteristics and roles that are common in sexually addicted families. However, each ACSA's story may differ. Using the framework we've outlined to name and describe their own story, ACSAs can unburden their shame without feeling the need to perfectly fit into anyone else's story or any suggested recovery tasks in this book. If we have used a phrase or made a recommendation that feels too strong or too soon to implement, ACSAs can adjust accordingly so that they can personalize their own recovery to their pace.

  Perfectionism is a common defense against carrying shame, *that is, If I can be perfect in my healing, then maybe I won't feel my shame.* There is no need for ACSAs to use perfection as a guide in their recovery from sexual shame; quite the opposite, ACSAs should learn to permit mistakes and imperfection. Wearing their recovery as a loose and comfortable shirt, not a restrictive jacket, helps. However, don't let this become a gateway to indecision or ambivalence. Along the way, ACSAs' recovery journeys will require clear and firm positions. They must be prepared to make them when the situations arise. And, they must give themselves permission to circle back with someone if they made a compromise or decision that was not in their best interests.

• **Identify major characteristics and ACSA role(s)**—There may be crossover in the roles ACSAs have played. They must get to know the primary role they played in their family, as they may have played more than one role, and characteristics of one may share similar ones with another. The critical recovery task for ACSAs is to recognize when they are beginning to act out the role that leads to relapsing back into the family drama. That is the moment to step back and give themselves a choice as to whether that response or decision is in their best interests. ACSAs must learn to "talk to that part of themselves" and express compassion for the bind they were in, and then, as their own caring, wise selves, give that part permission to break free from the role and act with choice.

ACSAs often confuse their identities or sense of selves with the roles they've played in their family. The Comforter and Caretaker may see herself as having her value and identity exclusively tied to caring for others, only to find herself attached to problematic people, and with self-neglect as a way of life. During times of crisis, all families will create roles of survival and coping methods until the crisis is over. Then, usually, the families move out of coping mode, and each member can re-emerge into their "true" selves. In ACSAs' families, the roles are more rigid and stuck in place in order to cope with the ongoing denial of sexual betrayals, secrets, and family discord. ACSAs must discover their true selves and move out of blindly acting out these roles!

ACSAs must notice the prominent ACSA characteristics that commonly emerge in their lives and trigger problematic patterns of behavior. It's helpful for them to become curious as to why the characteristics keep re-emerging and when they first began in their lives, and then to invite themselves into new choices. ACSAs are not defined by these characteristics. They must work to soften, contain, or alter the characteristics that cause them distress and trauma.

- **Release shame**—Learning to leave behind the family shame associated with sex addiction is the obvious core task of recovery for ACSAs. Earlier, we used the term "disinheriting" themselves from their families' sexual shame. For some, that may seem too strong a word, but it is the feeling needed to unburden themselves from the shame. They inherited the shame, through no choice of their own, from the apparent shamelessness often seen with sexual addiction. It is not their shame, and it is critical to "leave it behind" with the addict.

    Also, it is important to look at the role the other parent (spouses/partners of the sex addicts) played in ACSAs' sexual shame and struggles with intimacy. These parents may have been the primary messengers in delivering the shaming of ACSAs' sexuality. In reacting to the sex addicts, the other parents may have projected shame about sexuality onto the ACSAs as a means to control them, given that they felt unable to control the addicts' behaviors. This unwelcomed shame is confusing to the ACSAs and contributes to their carried, inherited shame. These other parents may also have turned to the ACSAs for emotional support, treated them like Surrogate Spouses, and/or guilted them into an alliance against the addicted parents. All this adds to the layers of shame and intimacy issues for ACSAs. The ACSAs must also be willing to confront, reconcile, and sort the feelings and issues with these parents. Some of the suggestions regarding boundaries we have made about how to deal with the sexually addicted parents can also be used with the other parents as well.

In addition, ACSAs must identify the negative core beliefs associated with the inherited sexual shame. They can picture that part of themselves and "have an internal conversation" with that part—encouraging themselves to leave the shame and negative beliefs about their sexuality, intimacy, bodies, or gender behind in the family home. Finally, they must affirm new beliefs that permit love, curiosity, freedom, and playfulness to take up space where the sexual shame once resided. We suggest ACSAs practice this internal conversation daily until it feels familiar and becomes a part of them. If their behavior, sexual or otherwise, is violating their values and/or hurting someone else, they are likely adding to their carried family shame. They must face this behavior, take responsibility, and be prepared to make changes.

• **Face their addictions**—Common to ACSAs are their own addictive behaviors used to soothe pain and sadness, discharge or contain anger, and/or create a sense of "aliveness" in the face of numbness and feelings of depersonalization. If they, themselves, are engaging in sexual or other addictive behaviors, it will be difficult to hold their parents to account for their own sex addiction.

Addiction hallmarks include compulsion, loss of control, and the inability to stop the behavior despite negative consequences. ACSAs with their own addictions must seek assistance from a qualified professional who understands addiction can be a primary disorder that needs addiction treatment protocols, as opposed to only seeking understanding of its underlying causes as the route to recovery. Avoid professionals who "don't believe in addiction." This position is at odds with the growing evidence that documents addiction for what it is, a primary disorder that requires specific treatment. Not "believing in it" may be a personal bias on the part of the professional that could prevent ACSAs' successful recoveries.

- **Grieve losses**—Recovery from ACSAs' roles will invariably bring changes to their relationships with family, friends, romantic partners, and even their children if they are parents. Some of these relationships will not endure the changes and the emergence of the "authentic selves" their recoveries create. Friendships they thought were close may find a need for greater separation and distance. Family members who seemed always aligned may turn on them. ACSAs may long for more satisfying romances, only to find that their choices of partners may have been rooted in the devalued part of themselves created by their families' sexual shame.

  ACSAs must be prepared to come to terms with the grief associated with their losses from change along the recovery path. They must learn to feel their feelings, be compassionate and patient with themselves, make peace with the changes, and find the courage to re-emerge with new choices on the other side of their grieving. And, most critically, they must be prepared to grieve the losses of the idealized families they thought they had and/or hoped to have. Without coming to terms with this loss, the tendency to fall back into old ACSA roles and family dysfunction will remain a strong likelihood.

- **Establish new values regarding their sexuality, gender, and body**—The sexual shame, rigid gender stereotypes, and preoccupation with body appearances (including critical and sexualized comments), all common in sexually addicted families, leaves ACSAs in conflict with their own bodies, genders, and sexuality. Out of this conflict comes a set of values, feelings, and perceptions about sexuality that reflects the inherited and carried shame from their family systems. ACSAs may be hypersexualized or find sexuality frightening, unimportant, or at the extreme, repulsive. They may overfocus on their appearances or neglect basic hygiene and grooming. And, they may feel inadequate and insecure in their sense of being men, women, or nonbinary people, either overcompensating with bravado or remaining in diminished roles.

Thus, it is important that they begin to "leave behind" this set of values, feelings, and perceptions in the homes they grew up in, and begin to create and welcome their own values about sexuality, gender, and their bodies. One helpful tool is to take out a sheet of paper and draw a line down the middle. On one side, list the negative sexually addicted family values that were inherited regarding sex, gender, and body image. Next to each, ACSAs can create a new value or hope that they can begin to invite into the core of their true selves. For example, "Sex is dirty and sinful" can become "Sex can be loving and playful." Or "I have to dress a certain way to be loved and wanted" can become "I can dress in the way that feels good to me and affirms the most loving sense of myself." They can imagine that part that carries the shameful messages and offer compassion and understanding that they feel seen, and then invite themselves to consider these new values, always reassuring that they will go at a pace that feels safe. We suggest ACSAs practice this daily until it feels familiar and normal to have a new set of love-, body-, and sexuality-affirming values.

RELATIONSHIPS, ROMANCE, SEX, AND DATING

ACSAs will need to chart a new course in relationships, one that reflects and contains the new values emerging in recovery. Leaving behind the compulsory role assignments means learning to navigate relationships in a new way that holds both empathy for others and a clear sense of commitment to their own needs, wants, and desires. We recall one individual saying it this way when reorganizing his commitment to himself in relation to his romantic partner: "I am committed to you, to us, and most importantly, to me." A lot can be taken from this. He is validating, first, the loyalty to his partner and the relationship, and he ends with the critical loyalty—the commitment to himself. This serves as the foundation that enables him to offer a clear commitment to others. If his romantic partner is in her (or his) adult self, then she welcomes this and feels reassured by the way he arranges his commitments. For ACSAs, this short and powerful declaration can be a compass point for relationships with family, friends, and lovers.

As ACSAs are letting go of their compulsory ACSA role assignments and sexual shame and embracing new values, they must consider the following when dating and establishing romance:

- **Go slow**—ACSAs often have histories of entering romance quickly as a way to "get past" the discomfort of sexual shame and try to feel "normal." This impetuousness often fails to take into account the process of "vetting," over time, if potential partners are right for them. If their partners are unwilling to go slow, perhaps they are not right for them. ACSAs must hold true to their values so that their new self-affirming commitments keep them on the paths that offer the best chances for successful romances.

- **Be playful, and stay away from gamesmanship**—Sex and love in ACSAs' families were used as commodities to be leveraged, bargained, or withheld. Further, sex was used to dominate and control. ACSAs learned that sex and love was a matter of who won and lost in the gamesmanship of the romantic dance. ACSAs must learn to be playful and sexual for love's sake and to express their own "inner lover" to their beloved—not to dominate or control, but to embrace and affirm.

- **Make safe bonding as important as being sexual**—Feeling emotionally and sexually safe in sexually addicted families was a casualty. Thus, ACSAs may value "good sex" in a relationship over whether they feel emotionally safe or not. To be clear, while there is nothing wrong with "good sex," ACSAs may fail to consider emotional safety factors and find themselves in volatile or harmful relationships. Or they may overvalue the need to feel safe so greatly that they find themselves in relationships that lack sexual passion. Here, sex is so shameful or frightening that they choose relationships that feel safe but are not particularly passionate. Learning to bring these two aspects together will help ACSAs feel both safe and sexual. They will feel free to be vulnerable, play sexually, and choose wisely.

- **Learn to "make love in and out of the bedroom"**—ACSAs, coming from families that model sexual extremes, expect themselves to be sexual athletes in the bedroom and fail to understand that learning to "make love" out of the bedroom is the best aphrodisiac for initiating and maintaining sexual passion. Being loving, romantic, playful, and emotionally vulnerable out of the bedroom invites the "letting go" into, and surrender to, sexual passion in the bedroom.

HOW TO MANAGE FAMILY INTERACTIONS

ACSAs' recoveries will invariably change the way they relate to their families. While we hope this new relationship dynamic brings them relief and a sense of empowerment, it is likely to also be filled with tension and pressure from family members to "go back to the way they were." In their newfound freedom, they may be tempted to confront and challenge their families, demand change, or avoid them altogether. While there may be a time to confront the truth with the sex addict, it should be done carefully and with the understanding that ACSAs are going to say the truth without expecting any change. Ideally this "truth telling" should be vetted and supported by a trained therapist. Often, ACSAs have taken on the responsibility to confront the truth in the family only to find themselves scapegoated and seen and treated as the problem.

Avoidance as a primary strategy may be needed when the situation is so toxic that it is not possible to be around the addicts or their families. This too should be carefully sorted with a trained therapist. If this option is taken, they should expect loss and grief, as well as finding the safety they seek. Having a period of time away from their families to settle into their recovery processes and to be clear on where they stand can be a helpful strategy in early recovery and during times of high stress. Being clear, direct, and diplomatic with their families in announcing this break is a useful approach. ACSAs must be prepared for pushback, guilt messages, and possible verbal attacks from family members. Another helpful tool is role-playing their messages with an empty chair or a friend and seeking support before and after.

A strategic approach, if having ongoing interactions with their families, includes identifying and setting boundaries that will keep ACSAs safe and out of their obligatory role assignments. Some individuals recovering from the impact of another's problematic or hurtful behavior have misused the concept of boundaries by exercising them to control, punish, and manage others. This is not the purpose of boundaries. Boundaries, while concerning another's behavior, are limits that ACSAs have placed on themselves. So, instead of announcing to their sex addict fathers, "My boundary is that I want you to stop saying sexual jokes about women in front of me," it becomes, "I feel uncomfortable when you make sexual jokes about women in front of me. If you are going to continue, I will need to leave." Or with their mothers who draw them into an alliance against their fathers, complaining about him to them, "Mom, I am uncomfortable with listening to you complain about Dad. If you continue to do that, I will need to end the conversation." In both examples, the boundaries reflect ACSAs' limits that they place on themselves rather than threats designed to control their parent.

Finally, ACSAs can make a list of boundaries they need for themselves, role-play their boundaries with an empty chair or a friend, list potential verbal assaults or guilt messages that will come from their families, and prepare a simple response statement for each possibility. It is also helpful for ACSAs to seek support before and after family visits.

THERAPY AND SUPPORT GROUPS

Choosing a therapist is an important and critical step for ACSAs to help in their recovery journey. First, a word on who ACSAs should not see—a therapist who willingly proclaims, "I don't believe in sex addiction." While there is still some debate on criteria regarding out-of-control sexual behavior, growing evidence validates that individuals can lose control of their sexual behavior, cannot stop despite negative consequences, and meet the criteria seen with other addictive disorders. So, therapists proclaiming they "don't believe" likely hold a personal bias and likely will not be able to validate and empathize with ACSAs' experiences. ACSAs must move on to someone else.

In addition, there are growing numbers of therapists who understand and have been trained in treating sex addicts, partners of sex addicts, and Adult Children of Alcoholics (ACOA). However, none of these models of treatment speak directly to the experience we find with ACSAs. Further, imposing one of these models as an overlay of ACSAs' experiences may actually hinder their recovery progress. Those trained in sex addiction may push for empathy toward the sex addict too soon. The partner trauma/ betrayal model may assume your ACSA experience carries the same impact—it does not. Those who know ACOA issues may assume yours are closely aligned, which they are not. ACSAs must look for someone who is not "married" to their model of therapy and understands the concepts of intergenerational shame, sexually addicted family system dynamics, sex addiction, partner trauma caused by sex addiction, and how adult children can carry childhood wounds. Ideally, someone directly trained to work with ACSAs will be most able to help in recovery. Nonetheless, this type of training is just beginning.

While therapists specializing in ACSA issues will become more common and attuned to the ACSA story as a result of this book and other efforts, the following may help in choosing a therapist now. The therapist should be licensed with the state ACSAs reside in and have either a master's or doctorate degree, along with some understanding about how a parent's out-of-control sexual behavior has a lasting negative impact on the adult child. The following criteria may help decide if the therapist is right for ACSAs. Having one to three sessions is a reasonable time to determine if the fit is right.

The therapist should:

- Understand ACSA issues. If they don't, ask them to review this book. If they are unwilling, consider finding a different therapist to work with who is curious about the book's contents.

- Have the ability to listen and be empathic toward ACSAs' concerns.

- Have the ability to lead to insights and solutions that go beyond what a friend, coach, or clergy member would advise.

- Be able to help ACSAs feel hopeful and empowered to manage their challenges.

- Have the ability to challenge, when needed, in a way that invites rather than shames ACSAs into breaking through denying and rationalizing problems.

- Be able to collaborate with other professionals when additional expertise is needed.

Support groups for Adult Children of Alcoholics (ACOA) based on the 12-step philosophy have been immensely helpful for those who have grown up in alcoholic families. ACSAs who have had an alcoholic parent who was also a sex addict may not have felt comfortable telling the entire sexual story at ACOA meetings, in spite of their usefulness regarding the impact of alcoholism. ACSAs need their own meetings. Fortunately, these meetings are slowly beginning to take shape. See the Resource section for information about ACSA groups. ACSAs can ask for the guidelines for starting their own meetings, and get one started in their communities.

Please understand that 12-step meetings are not group therapy and should not be used that way. The support groups are designed for validation and support, not therapy. They are a complement to therapy and serve a vital purpose in reducing the sexual shame that will come from the sharing of and hearing others' stories. Also, while other groups like ACOA, Children of Addicts or Dysfunctional Families, or support groups at places of worship can be helpful, ACSAs need a place where the invitation is clear, and primary, to freely share their sexual shame. So, when possible, attend a meeting specifically designed around ACSA issues. Hiding the sexual shame under the blanket of another framework will only further the shame. ACSAS must find the best home for their stories. It is time to leave the unwanted legacy behind!

Chapter Eleven

Bill of Rights and Responsibilities

ACSA recovery holds many gifts and promises for happy, healthy, fulfilling lives. There are boundless opportunities to grow into a more meaningful sense of self and a purposeful life filled with healthy relationships. As ACSAs begin to understand and unravel the effects of the past, they build mature relationships with the self in the present. Challenges become opportunities for growth; they learn to "re-parent" their inner children, who are still longing for the love, protection, and guidance they didn't receive from their primary caregivers. Creating healthy boundary systems becomes a gift, allowing them to both protect and contain themselves. They learn what makes up identities of their own while cultivating daily growth and change. They create and live within value systems that are congruent with their core beliefs and the information they receive from their emotions and bodily sensations. They learn how to pay attention to their own needs, share thoughts and feelings relationally, and act on their own beliefs.

Having been victimized and disempowered in childhood, ACSAs must draw a clear line in the sand, marking the end of childhood entanglements and the beginning of the lives they choose for themselves. Healing the wounds caused by parental sex addiction is a decision that they must make each day: to live in the habituated unconscious patterns of the past or to forge new paths forward and choose their own ways into their chosen futures, new legacies of joy, freedom, and wholeness. These decisions mark the beginning of recovery. They are opportunities, one choice at a time, one day at a time, to cultivate new family legacies free from sexual shame. It requires a willingness to consistently move into, and through, difficult emotions, beliefs, and relational patterns, even (and especially) when doing so is painful. Without ongoing support, ACSAs are bound to repeat the patterns of the past or pass on dysfunctional patterns to the next generation.

The following chart holds a list of declarations of rights and responsibilities for recovering ACSAs. Because ACSAs were not taught this in their families of origin, it is common to need daily reminders. Thus, the following list can be recited out loud as a daily practice for changing old beliefs, or it can be recorded, in their own voices, and listened to daily until these truths take hold inside their hearts and become the foundations of their inner dialogues. There can be no negotiation of these rights. ACSAs are entitled to healing from family dysfunction and recovery of their sense of self, their values, and their inherent worth.

As they heal, ACSAs become responsible, attuned adults who feel equal to others and can express themselves authentically while also being mindful of the impact their thinking, feelings, and behaviors have on others. The ACSA Bill of Rights and Responsibilities reflects the "both/and" nature of recovery: They learn to both stand firm in the knowledge of their inherent worth as human beings and simultaneously become responsible for ensuring their own rights and valuing the rights of others. They take action toward their own long-term best interests, while also considering their impact on others. ACSAs have to be accountable to and for themselves. In recovery, they are moving into healthy, mature adult relationships with themselves and other people, where responsibilities are seen as *opportunities* for accountability and growth. In the past, family loyalties, obligations, and expectations crushed ACSAs' sense of selves, but in recovery, responsibilities are freely made choices that honor ACSAs' own values, goals, and human dignity.

ACSA Bill of Rights and Responsibilities

	RIGHTS	RESPONSIBILITIES
1	I have the right to live a life free from sexual shame.	It is my responsibility to do the work of releasing sexual shame that never belonged to me.

	RIGHTS	RESPONSIBILITIES
2	I have the right to feel safe in my body and define my own sexuality.	It is my responsibility to create a loving, healthy relationship with my body and sexuality.
3	I have the right to enjoy healthy, nurturing sexual and nonsexual touch in my relationships.	It is my responsibility to honor others' preferences regarding healthy, nurturing sexual and nonsexual touch.
4	I have the right to explore and create healthy thoughts, feelings, and values about my sexuality, free from judgment and shame.	It is my responsibility to embrace and honor the gift of my sexuality and its healthy expression within my value system.
5	I have the right to explore how my femininity, masculinity, or nonbinary identity were injured in my sexually addicted family.	It is my responsibility as an adult to create my own beliefs and values about what it means for me to be a woman, man, or nonbinary person.
6	I have the right to say "no" and to protect myself from unwanted sexual advances and authentic boundary violations.	It is my responsibility to learn and create healthy boundary systems to protect and contain my body, sexuality, thinking, feelings, and behavior.

	RIGHTS	RESPONSIBILITIES
7	I have the right to protect myself from interactions and relationships that are based only on emotional intensity rather than healthy intimacy.	It is my responsibility to learn and develop healthy skills in areas of emotional, intellectual, physical, sexual, and spiritual intimacy.
8	I have the right to initiate adult relationships that are honest, nurturing, supportive, safe, and personally fulfilling.	It is my responsibility to determine the level of intimacy and vulnerability I am comfortable with in my relationships and communicate this information directly.
9	I have the right to learn what authentic trust is in my relationship with self and others.	It is my responsibility to notice the impact my behavior has on my relationship with self and others.
10	I have the right to choose relationships that support my highest good and let go of relationships that undermine me.	It is my responsibility to set healthy boundaries that assist me in feeling safe and balanced in my relationships with others.
11	I have the right to live my life free from inappropriate guilt, toxic loyalties, and burdensome obligations to my parent(s).	It is my responsibility to return my parents' burdens to them, become loyal to myself, my partner of choice, and my family of procreation.

	RIGHTS	RESPONSIBILITIES
12	I have the right to be treated with respect in my family, without being blamed, shamed, intimidated, or scapegoated.	It is my responsibility to set and honor my own boundaries and values, and to protect myself from family members who continue to behave shamelessly.
13	I have the right to request information, a formal disclosure, amends, and/ or emotional restitution from my parent(s) as to how I was impacted by their choices and behavior.	I have the responsibility to determine what level of interaction and information is best for me in this process and to accept others' decisions about their participation.
14	I have the right to a community of recovery and to competent, professionally trained clinicians who understand the legacy and burdens to be healed from growing up in a family with a sexually addicted parent.	It is my responsibility to seek out the help and support I need to heal, and to advocate for myself and other ACSAs when needed.

15	I have the right to heal from the wounds inflicted by my sexually addicted family.	It is my responsibility to understand this family legacy began long ago, and I can only change one person—me.

The gift of recovery is that we have the opportunity to create the lives we want and have always deserved. We free ourselves from carrying our families' fear, pain, anger, and shame. We forge a new path where we are both safe and free. We did not choose the family legacy that we were given in childhood, but we can accept and understand it. We can heal the wounds that have been festering for generations by digesting the pain, transforming it into healing, integrating it into ourselves, and finally, finding an appropriate place for it in the whole of who we are. We do not let the legacy of the past define us but choose to overcome it by dismantling its parts and using them to build something new, something better, a life in which we are happy and whole. We no longer keep secrets. We use our voices to heal. We no longer hide our shame. We let the light in. When we do the work of recovery, we honor our parents, our ancestors, our future families, and ourselves with a new family legacy of compassion, transformation, and truth.

Journal Reflections

We hope that *A Light in the Dark* has helped you understand the specific trauma of living with a sex-addicted parent and revealed the patterns of dysfunction and how they may have impacted your life. Moreover, we trust that the stories and advice shared within will inspire you to find a path to healing.

Undoubtedly, the book has stirred memories and emotions. Please use the following pages to reflect on your feelings and insights that have emerged from your reading of the book. Take your reflections to your therapist and support groups for counsel and support.

—*In light and healing, Ken, Mary, and Culle*

Describe the major impact that growing up in a sexually addicted family has had on you?

_____

_____

_____

_____

_____

_____

_____

_____

_____

_____

_____

_____

FOR TODAY, I will do the following to help my recovery as an ACSA:

_____

_____

_____

_____

_____

What secrets do you carry from your sexually addicted family and how have they impacted you?

_____

_____

_____

_____

_____

_____

_____

_____

_____

_____

_____

_____

FOR TODAY, I will do the following to help my recovery as an ACSA:

_____

_____

_____

_____

_____

What was your first discovery of (or exposure to) sex addiction in your family?

_____

_____

_____

_____

_____

_____

_____

_____

_____

_____

_____

_____

FOR TODAY, I will do the following to help my recovery as an ACSA:

_____

_____

_____

_____

_____

What messages do you carry about sexuality and/or gender that came from your sexually addicted family? How do you struggle with these today?

_____

_____

_____

_____

_____

_____

_____

_____

_____

_____

_____

_____

FOR TODAY, I will do the following to help my recovery as an ACSA:

_____

_____

_____

_____

_____

What did you learn about love and romantic relationships in your sexually addicted family? How do you struggle in relationships today?

_____

_____

_____

_____

_____

_____

_____

_____

_____

_____

_____

_____

FOR TODAY, I will do the following to help my recovery as an ACSA:

_____

_____

_____

_____

_____

Describe the role(s) you play that developed from your sexually addicted family.

_____

_____

_____

_____

_____

_____

_____

_____

_____

_____

_____

_____

_____

FOR TODAY, I will do the following to help my recovery as an ACSA:

_____

_____

_____

_____

_____

_____

Did you align with one parent in your sexually addicted family? Why?
If not, why not?

_____

_____

_____

_____

_____

_____

_____

_____

_____

_____

_____

_____

FOR TODAY, I will do the following to help my recovery as an ACSA:

_____

_____

_____

_____

_____

Describe how family relationships get in the way of your happiness as an adult.

_____

_____

_____

_____

_____

_____

_____

_____

_____

_____

_____

FOR TODAY, I will do the following to help my recovery as an ACSA:

_____

_____

_____

_____

_____

What do you want your sexuality and/or gender to mean to you today as an adult?

_____

_____

_____

_____

_____

_____

_____

_____

_____

_____

_____

_____

_____

FOR TODAY, I will do the following to help my recovery as an ACSA:

_____

_____

_____

_____

_____

_____

What do you want a healthy relationship/partnership to mean to you?

_____

_____

_____

_____

_____

_____

_____

_____

_____

_____

_____

FOR TODAY, I will do the following to help my recovery as an ACSA:

_____

_____

_____

_____

_____

_____

Resources

Adult Children of Alcoholic/Dysfunctional Families
www.adultchildren.org

Adult Children of Sex Addicts (ACSA)
www.cosa-recovery.org
go to: https://cosa-recovery.org/meeting/adult-children-of-sex-addicts-acsa-onl-48/2022-03-15/

Al-Anon
www.al-anon.org

Alateen
www.al-anon.alateen.org

Alcoholics Anonymous
www.aa.org

Codependents Anonymous (CODA)
www.coda.org

Codependents of Sexual Addiction (COSA)
www.cosa-recovery.org

National Association for Children of Alcoholics (NACOA)
www.nacoa.org

National Organization Against Male Sexual Victimization
www.malesurvivor.org

Overeaters Anonymous
www.oa.org

Recovering Couples Anonymous
www.recovering-couples.org

S-Anon (Partners)
www.sanon.org

Sex Addicts Anonymous (SAA)
www.saa-recovery.org

Sexaholics Anonymous
www.sa.org

Sex and Love Addicts Anonymous (SLAA)
www.slaafws.org

Bibliography

Adams, K. M. (2011). *Silently Seduced, Revised and Updated: When Parents Make Their Children Partners.* Health Communications, Inc.

Adams, K. M., & Alexander, M. (2007). *When He's Married to Mom: How to Help Mother-Enmeshed Men Open Their Hearts to True Love and Commitment.* Simon and Schuster.

Bass, E., & Davis, L. (1988). *The Courage to Heal: A Guide for Women Survivors of Child Sexual Abuse.* Random House.

Beattie, M. (1987). *Codependent No More: How to Stop Controlling Others and Start Caring for Yourself.* Harper & Row.

Bercaw, B., & Ginger. (2010). *The Couple's Guide to Intimacy: How Sexual Reintegration Therapy Can Help Your Relationship Heal.* California Center for Healing.

Bergstrom, J. (2019). *Gifts from a Challenging Childhood: Creating a Practice for Becoming Your Healthiest Self.* Mountain Stream Publishing Company.

Black, C. (1987). *It Will Never Happen to Me!* Ballantine Books.

Black, C. (1999). *Changing Course: Healing from Loss, Abandonment, and Fear (2nd ed.).* Hazelden Foundation.

Black, C. (2018). *Unspoken Legacy: Addressing the Impact of Trauma and Addiction Within the Family.* Central Recovery Press.

Bradshaw, J. (1988). *Healing the Shame That Binds You.* Health Communications, Inc.

Bradshaw, J. (1988). *Bradshaw On: The Family: A New Way of Creating Solid Self-Esteem.* Health Communications, Inc.

Brown, N. (2001). *Children of the Self-Absorbed: A Grownup's Guide to Getting Over Narcissistic Parents.* New Harbinger Publications.

Carnes, P. (1997). *The Betrayal Bond: Breaking Free of Exploitative Relationships.* Health Communications, Inc.

Carnes, P. (1983). *Out of the Shadows: Understanding Sexual Addiction.* Hazelden Publishing.

Carnes, P., & Adams, K. (2020). *Clinical Management of Sex Addiction: Second Edition.* Routledge.

Carnes, S. (2020). *Courageous Love: A Couples Guide to Conquering Betrayal.* Gentle Path Press.

Caudill, J., & Drake, D. (2019). *Full Disclosure: How to Share the Truth After Sexual Betrayal.* Independently Published.

Caudill, J., & Drake, D. (2019). *Your Disclosure Document: A 10-Step Guide for Preparing Your Disclosure Document.* Independently Published.

Caudill, J. & Drake, D. (2021). *Full Disclosure: Seeking Truth After Sexual Betrayal–Volume Two for Partners: Preparing for Disclosure on Your Terms.* Independently Published.

Chopra, D. (1993/1994). *The Seven Spiritual Laws of Success: A Practical Guide to the Fulfillment of Your Dreams.* Amber-Allen Publishing.

Cohen, B. (2019). *I Love You, More: Short Stories of Addiction, Recovery, and Loss from the Family's Perspective.* (n.p.).

Conquest, W. (2013). *Letters to a Sex Addict: The Journey Through Grief and Betrayal.* CreateSpace Independent Publishing Platform.

Conquest, W., & Drake, D. (2017). *Letters from a Sex Addict: My Life Exposed.* CreateSpace Independent Publishing Platform.

Corley, M. D., & Schneider, J. P. (2002). *Disclosing Secrets: What, to Who, and How Much to Reveal.* Gentle Path Press.

Forward, S. (2002). *Toxic Parents.* Bantam Books.

Friel, J., & Friel, L. D. (1988). *Adult Children: Secrets of Dysfunctional Families.* Health Communications, Inc.

Gartner, R. B. (2005). *Beyond Betrayal: Taking Charge of Your Life After Boyhood Sexual Abuse.* Wiley & Sons.

Gottman, J., & Silver, N. (1999). *The Seven Principles for Making Marriage Work.* Three Rivers Press.

Hendrix, H. (2001). *Getting the Love You Want: A Guide for Couples.* Owl Books.

Hunter, M. (1997). Characteristics of the Members of the 12-Step-Based Self-Help Group Adult Children of Sex Addicts. *Sexual Addiction & Compulsivity* 4, no. 2, pages 169–177, Brunner/Mazel, Inc.

Katehakis, A. (2010). *Erotic Intelligence: Igniting Hot, Healthy Sex While in Recovery.* Health Communications, Inc.

Lee, J. (2001). *Growing Yourself Back Up: Understanding Emotional Regression.* Three Rivers Press.

Love, P., & Robinson, J. (1991). *The Emotional Incest Syndrome: What to Do When a Parent's Love Rules Your Life.* Bantam Books.

Maltz, W. (2001). *The Sexual Healing Journey: A Guide for Survivors of Sexual Abuse.* Harper Collins.

Mays, M. (2017). *The Aftermath of Betrayal.* Relational Recovery Press.

Mays, M. (2018). *When It All Breaks Bad: Ten Things to Do (and Not to Do) After Betrayal.* Relational Recovery Press.

Mellody, P., Miller, A. W., & Miller, J. K. (1989). *Facing Codependence: What It Is, Where It Comes From, How It Sabotages Our Lives.* Harper Collins.

Mellody, P., & Miller, A. W. (1989). *Breaking Free: A Recovery Workbook for Facing Codependence.* Harper Collins.

Mellody, P., Miller, & A. W., & Miller, J. K. (2003). *Facing Love Addiction: Giving Yourself the Power to Change the Way You Love.* Harper Collins.

Mellody, P., & Freundlich, L. S. (2003). *The Intimacy Factor: The Ground Rules for Overcoming the Obstacles to Truth, Respect, and Lasting Love.* Harper Collins.

McDaniel, K. (2021). *Mother Hunger: How Adult Daughters Can Understand and Heal from Lost Nurturance, Protection, and Guidance.* Hay House, Inc.

Real, T. (2008). *The New Rules of Marriage: What You Need to Know to Make Love Work.* Ballantine Books.

Schwartz, R. (2021). *No Bad Parts: Healing Trauma & Restoring Wholeness with the Internal Family System Model.* Sounds True.

Whitfield, C. (1989). *Healing the Child Within: Discovery and Recovery for Adult Children of Dysfunctional Families.* Health Communications, Inc.

Woititz, J. (1983). *Adult Children of Alcoholics.* Health Communications.

Acknowledgments

Frist, many thanks and deep appreciation to my co-authors, Mary and Culle, who together helped bring this book to fruition and to create one voice from three, never an easy task. And to Dr. Patrick Carnes, a friend and mentor who has shown the way so often toward a light in the darkness of sex addiction. To the International Institute of Trauma and Addiction Professionals, particularly my Certified Sex Addiction Therapist colleagues, I owe a deep debt of gratitude for your tireless efforts to bring healing to those impacted by sex addiction. Our community has always felt like my professional, intellectual, and spiritual home in the fight to do our part to help others keep their heads out of the proverbial sand of denial. Finally, to my wife, Cheryl, and son, Zach, who remind me always that love is possible for this ACSA.

—Ken Adams

*I*would like to express my sincerest gratitude to the following people: To my co-authors, Culle and Ken, thank you for sharing your light with me and with all ACSAs. Your vulnerability and bravery have been inspiring, and it has been an honor to work with you both. Thank you to the many teachers, mentors, and unseen beings who have guided and protected me along the way, and to all the anonymous people who have shared with me in the rooms I have been blessed to find on my journey. Thank you to my husband, Tim, for supporting me always and in all ways. Without you it would not have been possible for me to write this book. Thank you to my mom for sitting with me late at night when I was a child, for being the first person to encourage me to make meaning out of my pain and to do something useful with it. Thank you to my beautiful children for inspiring me to strive to be the mother you need, for providing me with the motivation for continued healing and the hope for all children to be free from the pain of sex addiction.

—Mary Meyer

*F*irst and foremost, I would like to thank my co-authors, Ken, and Mary, for the opportunity and privilege to write this book together. Ken, your guidance and experience from beginning to end was invaluable! And Mary, I am so grateful to have found a kindred spirit who felt as passionately as I did about the need to give a voice to the experiences of adult children of sex addicts around the world. I owe an enormous debt of gratitude to Pia Mellody. Your developmental trauma disorder model saved my life, especially your groundbreaking work on healthy versus carried shame, re-parenting younger parts of self, and learning how to hold the paradox of remaining equal in inherent value amid my imperfection. Thank you to the women and men who shared their experience, strength, and hope daily, and to the numerous teachers, mentors, colleagues, family members, friends, and clients who have been part of my spiritual journey of healing and love the last thirty-six years.

—Culle Vande Garde

The three of us would like to thank HCI, especially Christian Blonshine and Christine Belleris, for their enthusiasm, editing, and support in seeing *A Light in the Dark* for the impact we think it offers and for seeing it through the publication process in such a timely manner.

About the Authors

© Scot Orser

Kenneth M. Adams, PhD, CSAT-S, is a licensed psychologist and faculty member with the International Institute of Trauma and Addiction Professionals and the clinical director of Kenneth M. Adams and Associates in suburban Detroit, Michigan. He is the author of *Silently Seduced* and *When He's Married to Mom* as well as co-editor of *Clinical Management of Sex Addiction: Second Edition*. Dr. Adams is the creator and director of overcomingenmeshment.com workshops. For more on Dr. Adams, visit www.drkenadams.com or Dr. Ken Adams on YouTube.

Mary E. Meyer, PhD, LMFT, CSAT, is executive director at Full Heart Family Therapy in Ankeny, Iowa. She is a Licensed Marital and Family Therapist, Certified Sex Addiction Therapist, and a Developmental and Relational Trauma Therapist. Dr. Meyer is dedicated to helping families heal from the effects of sex addiction and intergenerational family trauma. For more on Dr. Meyer visit, www.fullheart familytherapy.com.

© Shutterfly

Culle L. Vande Garde, LCSW-S, CSAT, is a licensed therapist, workshop facilitator, and speaker specializing in the treatment of Adult Children of Sex Addicts, Betrayal Trauma, Childhood Trauma, and Codependence. She is the founder and clinical director of Dallas Center for Relational Healing, serving individuals, couples, and families. For more on Culle, visit www.CulleVandeGarde.com.